Analytical Approaches Used in Stream Benthic Macroinvertebrate Biomonitoring Programs of State Agencies in the United States

By James L. Carter, U.S. Geological Survey; and Vincent H. Resh, University of California–Berkeley

Open-File Report 2013–1129

U.S. Department of the Interior
U.S. Geological Survey

U.S. Department of the Interior
SALLY JEWELL, Secretary

U.S. Geological Survey
Suzette M. Kimball, Acting Director

U.S. Geological Survey, Reston, Virginia: 2013

For more information on the USGS—the Federal source for science about the Earth,
its natural and living resources, natural hazards, and the environment—visit
http://www.usgs.gov or call 1–888–ASK–USGS

For an overview of USGS information products, including maps, imagery, and publications,
visit *http://www.usgs.gov/pubprod*

To order this and other USGS information products, visit *http://store.usgs.gov*

Suggested citation:
Carter, J.L., and Resh, V.H., 2013, Analytical approaches used in stream benthic macroinvertebrate
biomonitoring programs of State agencies in the United States: U.S. Geological Survey Open-File
Report 2013-1129, 50 p.

Contents

Figures

Tables

Conversion Factors

Inch/Pound to SI

Multiply	By	To obtain
Length		
foot (ft)	0.3048	meter (m)
Flow rate		
cubic foot per second (ft^3/s)	0.02832	cubic meter per second (m^3/s)

SI to Inch/Pound

Multiply	By	To obtain
Length		
meter (m)	3.281	foot (ft)
kilometer (km)	0.6214	mile (mi)
Area		
square kilometer (km^2)	247.1	acre
square kilometer (km^2)	0.3861	square mile (mi^2)
hectare (ha)	0.003861	square mile (mi^2)
Volume		
cubic meter (m^3)	35.31	cubic foot (ft^3)
cubic meter (m^3)	1.308	cubic yard (yd^3)
Flow rate		
meter per second (m/s)	3.281	foot per second (ft/s)
cubic meter per second (m^3/s)	35.31	cubic foot per second (ft^3/s)
cubic meter per day (m^3/d)	35.31	cubic foot per day (ft^3/d)
Mass		
kilogram (kg)	2.205	pound avoirdupois (lb)

Abbreviations and Acronym

ABBREVIATIONS AND ACRONYMS	MEANING
CWA	Clean Water Act
FFG	Functional feeding group
MMI	Multimetric index
O/E	Observed divided by expected
%	percent
QA/QC	Quality assurance and quality control
SD	Standard deviation
TMDL	Total maximum daily load
USEPA	U.S. Environmental Protection Agency
USGS	U.S. Geological Survey

Analytical Approaches Used in Stream Benthic Macroinvertebrate Biomonitoring Programs of State Agencies in the United States

By James L. Carter[1], and Vincent H. Resh[2]

Abstract

Biomonitoring programs based on benthic macroinvertebrates are well-established worldwide. Their value, however, depends on the appropriateness of the analytical techniques used. All United States State, benthic macroinvertebrate biomonitoring programs were surveyed regarding the purposes of their programs, quality-assurance and quality-control procedures used, habitat and water-chemistry data collected, treatment of macroinvertebrate data prior to analysis, statistical methods used, and data-storage considerations. State regulatory mandates (59 percent of programs), biotic index development (17 percent), and Federal requirements (15 percent) were the most frequently reported purposes of State programs, with the specific tasks of satisfying the requirements for 305b/303d reports (89 percent), establishment and monitoring of total maximum daily loads, and developing biocriteria being the purposes most often mentioned. Most states establish reference sites (81 percent), but classify them using State-specific methods. The most often used technique for determining the appropriateness of a reference site was Best Professional Judgment (86 percent of these states). Macroinvertebrate samples are almost always collected by using a D-frame net, and duplicate samples are collected from approximately 10 percent of sites for quality assurance and quality control purposes. Most programs have macroinvertebrate samples processed by contractors (53 percent) and have identifications confirmed by a second taxonomist (85 percent). All States collect habitat data, with most using the Rapid Bioassessment Protocol visual-assessment approach, which requires ~1 h/site. Dissolved oxygen, pH, and conductivity are measured in more than 90 percent of programs. Wide variation exists in which taxa are excluded from analyses and the level of taxonomic resolution used. Species traits, such as functional feeding groups, are commonly used (96 percent), as are tolerance values for organic pollution (87 percent). Less often used are tolerance values for metals (28 percent). Benthic data are infrequently modified (34 percent) prior to analysis. Fixed-count subsampling is used widely (83 percent), with the number of organisms sorted ranging from 100 to 600 specimens. Most programs include a step during sample processing to acquire rare taxa (79 percent). Programs calculate from 2 to more than100 different metrics (mean 20), and most formulate a multimetric index (87 percent). Eleven of the 112 metrics reported represent 50 percent of all metrics considered to be useful, and most of these are based on richness or percent composition. Biotic indices and tolerance metrics are most often

---

[1]U.S. Geological Survey, Menlo Park, California.

[2]Department of Environmental Science, Policy, and Management, University of California, Berkeley, California.

used in the eastern U.S., and functional and habitat-type metrics are most often used in the western U.S. Sixty-nine percent of programs analyze their data in-house, typically performing correlations and regressions, and few use any form of data transformation (34 percent). Fifty-one percent of the programs use multivariate analyses, typically non-metric multi-dimensional scaling. All programs have electronic data storage. Most programs use the Integrated Taxonomic Information System (75 percent) for nomenclature and to update historical data (78 percent). State procedures represent a diversity of biomonitoring approaches which likely compromises comparability among programs. A national-state consensus is needed for: (1) developing methods for the identification of reference conditions and reference sites, (2) standardization in determining and reporting species richness, (3) testing and documenting both the theoretical and mechanistic basis of often-used metrics, (4) development of properly replicated point-source study designs, and (5) curation of benthic macroinvertebrate data, including reference and voucher collections, for successful evaluation of future environmental changes.

Introduction

The evaluation of benthic macroinvertebrate assemblages for biological monitoring programs that assess the status of wadeable streams is now well-established in most States within the U.S. (Carter and Resh, 2001; U.S. Environmental Protection Agency, 2002). However, the similarities, differences, and comparability of biomonitoring results among the majority of States have not been described. Comparability among programs is influenced by variability in the field and laboratory methods used (Carter and Resh, 2001), as well as by variability in the methods used in data analysis (U.S. Environmental Protection Agency, 2002; Cao and Hawkins, 2011).

Although a detailed survey of the field and laboratory methods used by State programs has been completed (Carter and Resh, 2001), this present study represents the results of an identically constructed questionnaire-based survey to evaluate methods used for data analysis. This survey, like the survey by Carter and Resh (2001), also was done among U.S. State agency benthic biologists that use macroinvertebrates for assessing streams. The objectives of this article are to: (1) describe the purposes for which State agencies use bioassessments, (2) describe the analytical approaches currently in use by these programs, and (3) discuss the effects these choices potentially have on evaluating the status of streams being surveyed. Several previous studies have analyzed sampling and sorting methods used in benthic research and water-quality studies (for example, Winterbourn, 1985; Voshell and others, 1989; Resh and McElravy, 1993; Carter and Resh, 2001; U.S. Environmental Protection Agency 1996, 2002). However, this study represents the most recent questionnaire-based survey (compare U.S. Environmental Protection Agency, 1996, 2002) that summarizes the purposes and analytical methods used by U.S. State bioassessment programs using macroinvertebrates for biomonitoring streams.

Methods

The questionnaire for this survey (appendix 1) was designed to be identical to the questionnaire used previously by Carter and Resh (2001) to examine site selection, sampling, and sample-processing procedures. The present questionnaire consisted of six sections. The first section addressed the purpose of the State's biomonitoring program and its principal design. The second section addressed quality assurance and quality control (QA/QC). The third section addressed the collection of habitat data. The fourth section addressed the methods used for preparing macroinvertebrate data prior to analysis. The fifth section addressed the statistical calculations used in analyzing data. The sixth assessed aspects related to data storage.

Questions included Yes-No responses, multiple choice, and short fill-in responses. Some of the fill-in responses were unprioritized lists of items (for example, chemical constituents) and others were prioritized lists. The total number of responses in the unprioritized lists represented the total number of items listed; therefore, the response often exceeded the number of questionnaires received. Responses from prioritized lists typically were evaluated in two ways. First, the frequency of responses was tabulated. Second, responses were weighted by the priority that each program gave to a response. Weighting was linear; therefore, if a question asked respondents to prioritize from 1 to 5, the first priority was weighted by 5, the next highest priority by 4, and so on. For many questions, we requested respondents to provide additional comments and experiences.

We received responses from representatives of all 50 States; however, 3 States did not feel their programs were sufficiently well-established to submit details of their programs. Consequently, this survey represents a census of all viable State programs. State programs initially were contacted based on the list of participants used by Carter and Resh (2001). When changes in personnel responsible for such programs occurred (which was often), we contacted those currently involved in the State's bioassessment program. Programs were requested to submit one questionnaire detailing non-point-source study methods and one questionnaire detailing point-source study methods if different approaches were used. Toxicity testing [e.g., whole effluent toxicity (WET) testing (http://cfpub.epa.gov/npdes/wqbasedpermitting/wet.cfm) using macroinvertebrates was not evaluated.]

Results are based on the responses from all questionnaires, but percentages were calculated based on the number of responses to each specific question. Regional differences in methods were evaluated using frequency tables and were tested by Chi-square analyses by partitioning States based on regional location. Regions were defined as east and west of the Mississippi River. Statistical analyses were calculated by using STATISTICA 9.0 (Version 9.1210.0, StatSoft Inc., Tulsa, Okla.).

Results

Purpose of Program

The most important purpose each State listed for their biomonitoring program varied, but responses were most often related to addressing requirements of the Clean Water Act (CWA) (U.S. Government Accountability Office, 1989). Most (42/46, 91 percent) States rank addressing State regulatory mandates, the development of biotic indices, or satisfying Federal reporting responsibilities as their first priority (table 1). Fewer States list satisfying local regulations as important. Approximately 70 percent (33/47) of all States list research as an important component of their programs. The development of an O/E approach similar to the River Invertebrate Prediction and Classification System (RIVPACS; Wright and other, 2000), was on the "to do" list of approximately one-half (22) of all programs. Additional purposes that individual States list in the narrative descriptions of their programs include: public education and outreach, establishing and monitoring total maximum daily loads (TMDLs as defined by the CWA, Section 303(d) [i.e., "the maximum amount of a pollutant a waterbody can receive and still meet water quality standards and an allocation of that amount to the pollutant's source" (U.S. Environmental Protection Agency, 2002)]), identifying exceptional waterways, tracking the progress of restoration projects, developing site-specific standards, monitoring climate change, monitoring the effectiveness of non-point-source runoff watershed-improvement programs (Clean Water Act, Section 319), and assisting in enforcing water-quality standards. However, when responses were weighted by priority (see Methods section), which indicates importance, a different pattern emerged. Then, 41 percent of respondents listed State regulations, 22 percent listed Biotic Index development, 17 percent listed Federal regulations, 7 percent listed research, and 6 percent listed both listed local regulation and O/E development. Only one program explicitly stated that their biomonitoring program was non-regulatory.

An ordering also exists of the actual use of State monitoring results, which differed from the sequence of listed purposes. First, the dominant use of the monitoring data is for fulfilling Federal reporting requirements, with 89 percent (39/44) of State monitoring information used for generating the State and Federal biennial 305(b) report that, in part, details general water-quality conditions and highlights programs instituted to protect and restore waterbodies (Clean Water Act Section 305(b), Clean Water Act 35 U.S.C. § 1315(b)). All States but one plan to use the results of biomonitoring to fulfill this purpose by 2012. In addition, 87 percent (40/46) of the programs use their biological-monitoring programs for creating their State's biennial 303(d) (CWA 35 U.S.C. § 1313(d)) report that, in part, lists the State's impaired waters (Note: the 305(b) and 303(d) is now a single, integrated report). Four other States planned to have this function in place by 2012, as well.

The second most often stated use of data is for the establishment and monitoring of TMDLs for specific pollutants. Only a slight difference existed in the number of programs using analyses for establishing TMDLs (30/41, 73 percent) and in those using analyses for monitoring TMDLs (28/42, 67 percent). Most remaining programs (11–14) plan on using biomonitoring data in at least one aspect of the TMDL process by 2012.

The third most frequently listed use of data is for the establishment of biocriteria. Of the programs that have developed biocriteria, most (90/134, 67 percent) are narrative. Additional comments submitted by the States indicated a wide range in the degree of biocriteria development, from programs that did not know when these criteria would be established to programs that have had them in place for more than a decade.

The majority of respondents (35/43, 81 percent) indicate that they do not distinguish between point and non-point-source evaluations in the design of their studies, nor do they seem to modify the methods used for data preparation and analyses for these different types of studies. Some (7/39, 18 percent) programs did report using "upstream compared to downstream" designs with reference sites located upstream of the potential or assumed impact being tested (Green, 1979). Seven programs reported specifically restricting their analyses to non-point-source studies, and one State submitted a response that detailed the differences between point and non-point analyses.

Reference Condition

Most States (39/48, 81 percent) have established reference sites that are regionally specific. The number of sites per State varies, ranging from 12 to 200. Additionally, the factors used by individual States for partitioning their State into homogeneous physiographic settings also vary. Many of these factors are natural environmental factors (for example, altitude, land cover, and stream gradient) that can influence the potential fauna of a stream. To account for these influences, 91 percent (39/43) of State programs classify their reference sites into homogenous groups. The factors used for classifying sites, however, not only vary among States as stated above, but the importance of one factor compared to another also varies, with some factors being more commonly accounted for than others when reference conditions are defined (table 2). Choosing reference sites is a multistep process, and the first step almost always involves partitioning the State into similar regions based on categorical variables. Omernik's 1987 Level-III ecoregions (Omernik, 1987) is the most often referenced stratifying factor listed by State programs. When this factor is combined with other similar stratifying factors that were listed (for example, bioregions and physiographic regions), ecological regions clearly dominated the reference-site stratification approach used by State programs (table 2). GIS-derived land-cover information is used as a primary stratifying criterion (27/35, 77 percent) when reference sites are chosen. Other factors also used include basin area, land cover, elevation, and stream gradient.

Determination of whether a site should be included in a reference-site group also involves several steps. Once the programs partition their States into homogeneous areas by using the above criteria, approximately 76 percent determine whether the chosen reference sites are appropriate based primarily on three additional sources of information: physical, chemical, and Best Professional Judgment (BPJ). Inclusion or exclusion of a site is dependent on evaluating a site's physical-habitat data (27/35, 77 percent), chemical data (24/35, 69 percent), or by using a multivariate physiochemical index (9/35, 26 percent). BPJ is reported as being used more often (30/35, 86 percent) than any other factor; however, it is likely used in combination with physical-chemical factors.

Most State programs (31/41, 76 percent) reported that they use no information on macroinvertebrate distributions when identifying reference sites; however, eight programs evaluate the composition of macroinvertebrate assemblages when making a final decision as to whether a site should be considered a reference site.

Of all the State programs, 61 percent (28/46) have at least some reference sites in common with other bioassessment programs. Some of these programs (9/23, 32 percent) share sites with other State programs, but more commonly (24/25, 96 percent), reference sites are shared with Federal programs [for example, National Water-Quality Assessment Program (NAWQA), Environmental Monitoring and Assessment Program (EMAP), Wadeable Streams Assessment (WSA), and the National Rivers and Streams Assessment (NRSA)]

Sampling and Replication

Most programs (40/49, 82 percent) collect sample replicates, which most often are duplicate samples collected from a predetermined percentage of sites. The second sample is collected for QA/QC purposes. The percentage of sites from which these replicates are collected ranges from 5 percent to 20 percent (median=10 percent).

The D-frame net is the most widely used sampling device among programs. However, the techniques used for collecting macroinvertebrate samples using the D-frame net reported in this survey are highly variable, ranging from strictly qualitative to quantitative. Methods currently used include collecting from: a fixed area (for example, 1 m^2), a fixed effort (for example, a specified amount of time), an effort-limited fixed area, artificial substrates (Hester-Dendy), natural substrates (rock baskets), single habitats, and multiple habitats. There is approximately an equal number of programs that report sampling a fixed area (25) and sampling using a fixed effort (20). Six programs specifically state they collect a qualitative multihabitat sample instead of a quantitative sample.

Contractor Information

Macroinvertebrate samples must either be processed by in-house personnel or be sent out to be processed by contractors. Fifty-three percent (26/49) of State programs have samples either fully processed by contractors; or have the macroinvertebrates sorted by program personnel and then identified by contractors. Most of these programs receive raw taxonomic data from the contractor and analyze it themselves. However, six programs have contractors fully process samples, calculate metrics, and provide estimates of site condition.

Quality Assurance/Quality Control

To insure taxonomic accuracy, most programs (40/47, 85 percent) have the identification of taxa confirmed by a second taxonomist. This second taxonomist may be located in the laboratory that did the initial identification or at an outside laboratory. A variety of protocols have been established for confirming these identifications. Some programs (18) have a fixed percentage of their processed samples confirmed. Most often 10 percent of the samples are checked (range = 5–100 percent). In contrast, some programs (20/42, 48 percent) have individual taxa confirmed instead of entire samples. However, almost all of these latter programs (19/20, 95 percent) have taxa reviewed only when they are uncertain of their identification. Finally, three programs have their entire voucher and reference collections reviewed on an ongoing basis.

Of the 88 percent (43/49) of the programs that responded regarding the certification of the taxonomic expertise of those identifying macroinvertebrates, 28 percent (12/43) required Society for Freshwater Science (SFS) taxonomic certification [formerly North American Benthological Society (NABS) taxonomic certification—http://www.nabstcp.com/]. Some annotated responses regarding the need for taxonomic certification included: (1) "We do our own in-house certification because the NABS certification is insufficient"; (2) "Yes, but only for some projects"; (3) "I don't know"; and most often, (4) "We're planning on requiring NABS certification."

To insure the consistency of taxonomic identifications temporally and spatially, most programs (43/48, 90 percent) maintain reference collections. Only 83 percent (19/23) of programs that sort and identify samples in-house maintain reference collections themselves, whereas 96 percent (24/25) of programs that have samples processed by contractors maintain reference collections.

Habitat Information Collected

All programs indicate they collect at least some habitat data at the same sites where they collect macroinvertebrate samples. Fifty-six percent (26/46) of the programs use the Rapid Bioassessment Protocol (RBP) visual habitat assessment of Barbour and others (1999). Other protocols used include USEPA's EMAP, WSA, and NRSA. Some programs (18/46, 39 percent) use a habitat-assessment approach that is specific to their individual program. These protocols are sometimes based on procedures developed by State fisheries programs or State parks departments. Typically, regardless of its origin, the same protocol is used (42/44, 96 percent) throughout the State.

The time spent collecting physical-habitat data varies greatly among programs (fig. 1). In general, programs that answered "Yes" to using the RBP visual habitat assessment spend approximately 1 h per site collecting physical-habitat data. Those using other protocols spend more than twice as long (>2.5 h) per site. Some programs (11/35, 31 percent) obtain physical-habitat data from others, such as the fisheries portions of the State assessment program, local programs, contractors performing assessments, other State agencies, universities, and Federal programs.

In terms of specific types of physical information collected, most programs estimate water velocity (34/46, 74 percent) and either wetted depth and width (26 and 23, respectively) or both bankfull and wetted depth and width (12 and 16, respectively). Discharge is measured by most (32/45, 71 percent) programs. Fifty-seven percent of the programs (25/49) collect data on bed sediments. Twenty two programs do Wolman pebble counts, or use a similar measure; the number of pebbles evaluated for the former ranges from 50 to 400 (median = 100). Some programs also estimate embeddedness and record other estimates of substrate composition.

Most programs (42/44, 95 percent) measure at least some water-chemistry parameters at each site. Dissolved oxygen (45/48, 94 percent), pH (45/48, 94 percent), conductivity (46/48, 96 percent), hardness (30/47, 64 percent), and some nutrient concentrations (38/46, 83 percent) are the most frequently collected constituents. Practically all programs measure one or more chemical species of nitrogen and phosphorus, particularly those that have the potential to influence water quality. Water samples are analyzed for at least some metals by 16 of 33 States. Other constituents frequently measured include total suspended solids (TSS), dissolved organic carbon (DOC), SO_4^{-2}, and Cl^-. One-third of the programs (11/33, 33 percent) analyze turbidity.

A majority of the programs (35/47, 74 percent) access continuously collected physical or chemical data. The most frequently referenced source is USGS streamflow-gaging station data. The only other continuous data generally collected is temperature; however, it was generally collected only for specific studies.

Benthic Macroinvertebrate Data Preparation

Taxa not Evaluated

State programs restrict their analyses to organisms most commonly referenced as macroinvertebrates. Eight percent (4/48) of the programs reported analyzing all taxa collected. Of the 46 survey responses that indicated which taxa were not included in their analyses, 38 programs excluded at least the terrestrial insects. Other taxa excluded by 20 programs are semiaquatic, such as Collembola (8), Hemiptera (9), microcrustaceans (6), and mites (8). Nematodes (5) and non-benthic swimmers (2) also are excluded by some programs. Other invertebrate groups not identified by some programs include worms (3), surface dwellers (for example, Gerridae) (1), and in some instances decapods (3), Nematomorpha (horsehair worms) (2), insect pupae (3), and colonial invertebrates (for example, bryozoans) (1). One program also excludes taxa if they lack tolerance information about them.

Species Traits

Species traits, such as functional feeding groups (FFGs) and pollution-tolerance values, are used in almost all State programs (46/48, 96 percent). Information about these traits is derived from a variety of sources. For the identification of FFGs, Merritt and others (2008 and earlier editions) are referred to by more programs (30) than Barbour and others (1999) (19), or local expertise (18). Information on the habits of macroinvertebrates followed the same trend, with 23 of 51 referencing Merritt and others (2008), 14 referencing Barbour and others (1999), and 12 relying on local expertise. Habitat information is used less often but when it is, it is mostly (16/36, 44 percent) obtained from Merritt and others (2008).

Tolerance Values

Tolerance values generally are reported as total tolerance to pollution, tolerance to organic pollution, or tolerance to metals. Most tolerance scores reported by State programs refer to organic loading (41/47, 87 percent); fewer scores referenced total tolerance and metal tolerance, 13 percent (6/47) and 28 percent (13/47), respectively. The source of tolerance values also varied among programs. Local expertise accounted for 31 percent (29/95 total references) of the sources, followed by values reported by Barbour and others (1999) (26/95, 27 percent). Values reported by Hilsenhoff (1977, 1987, 1988, 1998) (12/95, 13 percent) and Lenat (1993) (9/95, 9 percent) were less commonly cited.

More than one-half of the respondents (25/44, 57 percent) do not assign a new tolerance value to a taxon that does not already have one. Of those that do, the most common approach (7/18, 39 percent) is to use the tolerance value of the next higher taxon (for example, using the tolerance value of Baetidae for the genus *Baetis*). Other methods and techniques of assigning tolerance values also are used. For example, a tolerance value of a particular genus is assigned by one program after 25 records of the genus are acquired, while another program calculates a weighted average of all "relevant" taxa in their database (i.e., taxa they use in later analyses). Other programs drop taxa from further calculations if there are no known tolerance values.

Rare Taxa

Although the occurrence of numerically, spatially, or temporally rare taxa is typical in benthic samples, 79 percent (37/47) of programs do not modify their data to account for influences these rare taxa may have on their analyses. Of the 10 programs that do modify their data, 3 define rare as a taxon that occurs in either too few samples or at too few sites. The minimum percentage occurrence reported was either 5 or 10 percent of sites.

Subsampling

Typically, large benthic samples (for example, ≥ 1 m^2) have too many organisms to cost-effectively sort and identify; as a result, the vast majority of programs (40/48, 83 percent) subsample to reduce these numbers. All programs but one, subsample by sorting a fixed count of organisms from their original samples. The size of fixed-count subsamples (number of individuals sorted per sample) ranges from 100 to 600 (table 3).

Because most programs randomly sort a fixed-count subsample, which itself is a form of rarefication (i.e., standardizing to the same number of organisms identified per sample), most programs generally do not further rarefy by using a computer program; however, 10 programs do further rarefy by computer after subsampling. Thirteen percent (6/47) of the programs indicate they do not sort samples randomly, but rather sort to maximize estimates of richness.

Because rare taxa often are underrepresented in the typical random fixed-sorting process, 54 percent (22/41) of programs include a step in processing whereby rare (typically large) taxa are sorted from the sample. However, there is little uniformity in how these organisms are acquired or how their information ultimately is used in later analyses. Some programs set a 5-min time limit on sorting rare taxa, while others have no set time limit.

Choice of Metrics

All State programs calculate metrics. The number calculated by an individual program ranges from 2 to 100 (mean = 20, median = 9.5) per State. Moreover, most programs (41/47, 87 percent) also calculate at least one multimetric index (MMI). The programs cited 112 different metrics (table 4); however, 11 of these 112 metrics (~10 percent) represent 50 percent of all the metrics reported by the State programs. Consequently, many States have metrics that are unique to their programs. For example, 67 percent (75/112) of all the metrics listed by the States are used by only one program.

Richness and percentage-composition metrics represent the most common metrics used (fig 2), and programs listed about equal numbers of each. In contrast, biotic indices, diversity indices, and measures of abundance are used less often. However, when metrics were weighted by priority, that is, by the importance assigned by the programs, richness metrics far out-weighed all other types of metrics (table 5). There was no difference in the importance of richness and percentage-composition metrics used in States east and west of the Mississippi River (Chi-square 1.04, df = 1, p = 0.308).

Metrics Considered Most Useful

Of the 10 different metrics listed by each state program as being those most useful for their needs (table 4), richness metrics overwhelmingly were most commonly cited, either as total taxon, EPT (Ephemeroptera, Plecoptera, Trichoptera), mayfly, or stonefly richness. Together, richness metrics composed 73 percent of the metrics identified by the programs as most useful. The most often cited metric was total taxon richness (17/40, 43 percent).

There were 34 different metrics listed among the top three within each program in terms of their usefulness (table 4). Of those top three, the most often listed metrics were total taxon richness and EPT richness.

When metrics were classified into measures of sensitivity and tolerance in contrast to function and habitat, there was an east-west difference (Chi-square 7.95, df = 3, p = 0.047). For example, Hilsenhoff's biotic index and measures of tolerance are used much more often in the east than the west (table 6). Conversely, functional feeding groups and habitat characteristics are used more often in the west.

Statistical Analyses

Not all programs (31/45, 69 percent) report performing any statistical analysis of their macroinvertebrate data. Of the programs that do, the most commonly used statistical tests include correlation and regression (17/35, 49 percent), followed by ANOVA (7) and t-tests (4). Of the 22 tests mentioned as the 5 most useful to State programs, the above 4 tests represented 81 percent of all responses. Less often mentioned explicitly was the use of nonparametric tests. There was no single commonly used statistical package reported by the programs.

Multivariate analyses

Multivariate analyses, such as classification and ordination, are used by slightly more than one-half (23/45, 51 percent) of the programs. The most frequently listed (41 percent, 9/22) ordination technique is non-metric multi-dimensional scaling (NMS), followed by correspondence analysis and principal components analysis. The most often listed measures of similarity used are Bray-Curtis (7) and Jaccard (2).

Transformations

In terms of transformations and weights that can be used to treat macroinvertebrate data prior to statistical analysis, the most common approach used by State programs is to not modify the data at all (14/41, 34 percent). When programs do modify data, they most often standardize by sample or site by calculating relative abundance of each taxon as a percentage of the total number of individuals in the sample. Data are less often modified by calculating log abundance, eliminating rare taxa, and (or) converting their data to presence-absence. When the top three approaches are examined, the pattern remains similar to the above, with the calculation of percentage abundance the most frequently used data manipulation.

Data Storage

All programs store their data in electronic format and, likewise, all have established databases. The most common database program used is Microsoft Access (23/28 of the programs that responded about databases). Other often used databases are: Environmental Data Analysis System (EDAS; Tetra Tech, http://www.edas2.com/), which was developed initially using Access (11); ORACLE (Oracle Corp., Redwood Shores, Calif.) (8); and U.S.EPA's STORET (3). Some programs report having developed customized databases. Eleven programs indicate they also store their data in spreadsheet format. Only one program stores their data in a flat file (= ASCII) format. Most programs (36/48, 75 percent) also maintain a hardcopy of their data. Only 25% (12/45) of the programs currently post their data on the Internet.

Most programs (30) primarily depend on the Integrated Taxonomic Information System (ITIS; http://www.itis.gov/) for their nomenclature, but many programs use, in conjunction with the ITIS, Merritt and others (2008). Some programs use regional, continent-wide, and other Web-based sources for nomenclature, as well.

Updating of Historical Data

Most programs (33) report updating their historical monitoring data. This can involve simply updating changes in nomenclature, and most (21/27, 78 percent) programs do this task. However, updates also can include the splitting or combining of taxa when taxonomic revisions occur or errors are found, and 81 percent (22/27) of programs report doing this. Although combining taxa can be straightforward and includes little to no laboratory effort, the splitting of taxa requires reviewing and re-identifying specimens. Because this is often a time-consuming task, few programs (13/27, 48 percent) reported doing this to historical samples.

Discussion

Ideally, there could be a single stream macroinvertebrate bioassessment method that would satisfy all State and Federal needs, be applicable at all spatial and temporal scales, and be functional for all types of stressors. This "holy grail" of biomonitoring however, is not likely to be achieved in the near future (Shapiro and others, 2008). States currently have programs that reflect their historical development, financial constraints, and monitoring priorities (Davies and Jackson, 2006). Maintenance of State-specific methods, in contrast to adopting a uniform national method, may reflect the likely loss of using long-term, consistently collected data within each State, and the perceived institutional cost of reorganizing to a nationally standardized set of methods.

Standardization of programs across States would have certain national advantages, such as a directly comparable nation-wide evaluation of stream health (U.S. Environmental Protection Agency, 2003; The H. John Heinz III Center for Science, Economics and the Environment, 2008; Diamond and others, 2012). However, the goal of nationally standardized protocols does not appear to be either a State or Federal priority [(but see National Environmental Methods Index efforts, https://www.nemi.gov/apex/f?p=237:1:4496253571008062)]. Nevertheless, it is likely that migrating to a standard set of methods is necessary for valid comparison of State data to be made (Cao and Hawkins, 2011).

In contrast to a nationally consistent method, several other approaches to improve comparability among State programs have been proposed recently. One approach is a comprehensive protocol for evaluating the critical elements of a State's bioassessment program (Yoder and Barbour, 2009), whereby decisions about the rigor, comparability, applicability, and validity of individual aspects of programs are made. Another method is the development of a conceptual model of impairment, the Biological Condition Gradient (BCG) which has the potential to identify comparable levels of impairment across regions (Davies and Jackson, 2006). Comparability also can be addressed by direct comparison of metrics and indices (Stribling, 2011) and (or) assessment endpoints (Diamond and others, 2012). The usefulness of these approaches has been evaluated conceptually (Cao and Hawkins, 2011).

Through our questionnaire we obtained a composite view of the analytical methods used by State bioassessment programs. Below we examine the similarities and differences among them and highlight what we believe are the potential consequences of these differences.

Purpose of Program

Most States primarily use biological monitoring for supporting State water-quality programs and complying with Federal mandates. Moreover, Federal reporting is among the most often cited use of study results generated by biological-monitoring programs. The Federal 303(d), 305(b), and 319 requirements are among the highest priority tasks for these large-scale State programs because they satisfy Federally mandated tasks with which States are required to comply, contribute to national and State water-quality evaluations, and likely represent substantial sources of funding (U.S. Environmental Protection Agency, 2003). Establishment and monitoring of TMDLs also is extremely important at the State level because the results are necessary for delisting impaired streams as part of the CWA Section 303(d) (National Research Council, 2001; Kenney and others, 2009).

Another often reported use of monitoring data is tracking the success of restoration projects. Post-restoration monitoring is a critical need because of the dearth of follow-up studies that evaluate the effectiveness of specific mitigations (Kondolf, 1995). Only through post-restoration monitoring can advances be made in the development and application of restoration techniques (for example, Purcell and others, 2002; Hornberger and others, 2009).

Biocriteria developed from bioassessment data are narrative and (or) numeric expressions that describe the desired biological condition (structure and function) of aquatic communities inhabiting waters of a designated aquatic-life use (U.S. Environmental Protection Agency, 2002), and they are necessary components of State biomonitoring programs (Barbour and others, 2000). Biocriteria are based on the numbers and kinds of organisms present and are an important regulatory tool for protecting aquatic systems from impacts (Kenney and others, 2009). The predominance of narrative over numeric criteria in State programs is likely because narrative criteria are easier to develop, may be more flexible to apply, and often are more easily understood (Barbour and others, 1999; Barbour and Yoder, 2000). Nevertheless, the ultimate goal is the development of numeric-based biological criteria (Yoder and Barbour, 2009). Numeric criteria would make the application of biocriteria more similar to many chemical-based water-quality criteria. Because MMIs and biotic indices are integral to many bioassessments, particularly for the development of biocriteria (Kenney and others, 2009), the development of these measures is one of the most common tasks listed by the State programs (44/46).

Assessment of point-source impacts is another function of State biomonitoring programs and it typically requires study designs that differ from those evaluating non-point-source impacts (Downes and others, 2002). Prior to the 1980s, when water quality evaluation was more effluent-based (National Research Council, 2001), many studies simply used an upstream-downstream type of statistical design (Green, 1979); some State programs continue to use this type of design today. There are likely several reasons for a reduced emphasis on using point-source designs in current programs. First, successful reductions in point-source impacts that occurred during the 1970s and 1980s (i.e., since the 1972 CWA) have reduced the need for such studies. Second, there has been a shift from effluent-based monitoring to ambient monitoring. For example, many of the State programs that have developed concurrently with national USEPA programs [e.g. EMAP, WSA, NRSA, NARS (national aquatic resource surveys)] have stressed non-point-source assessments, most often based on probabilistic designs. Last, the statistical design of most upstream-downstream studies is considered flawed (Underwood, 1997). As a result of an increasing emphasis on using bioassessment data for detecting impacts from Municipal Separate Storm Sewer Systems (MS4s), a greater need currently exists for developing these types of bioassessment designs (U.S. Environmental Protection Agency, 2010).

Sampling

The D-frame net remains the device most often used by State programs for collecting macroinvertebrates, as was reported earlier by Carter and Resh (2001). However, many different collecting methods have been developed for its use. The type of sampling device and how it is used strongly influences whether data can be reported as absolute density (number of individuals per unit area, which is rarely done), abundance per unit effort (such as catch per unit effort in fisheries), or relative values (for example, percentage of each taxon). Although most State programs report macroinvertebrate data in terms of relative abundance (that is, sample standardized), some aspects of the BCG method proposed by Davies and Jackson (2006) require estimates of density (individuals per unit area or volume) and biomass, which are quantitative estimates that rarely were reported as being done by the State programs in our survey.

Subsampling

Large samples (i.e., ≥ 1 m^2) typically have too many organisms to cost-effectively sort and identify. As a result, the vast majority of programs use a subsampling technique to reduce this effort. Our previous 2001 survey indicated that more than one-half of all programs limited their sorting to 100 organisms. Since then, there has been an increase in the average number of organisms sorted (table 3; fig. 4 in Carter and Resh, 2001). This represents a substantial increase in laboratory effort per sample since 2001. We can speculate that the increase in the numbers of organisms in a fixed count from 100 to 300–500 has been strongly influenced by whether a program collects samples as part of an EMAP, WSA, or NRSA program and (or) whether a program is collecting with the intent of performing O/E-types of analyses (for example, Western Center for Monitoring and Assessment of Freshwater Ecosystems, http://cnr.usu.edu/wmc/), because many of these programs or approaches suggest a minimum of a 300 organism subsample (Herlihy and others, 2008; Ode and others, 2008). Similar size fixed-count subsamples represent one step that can lead to more comparable richness estimates.

The ongoing debate regarding the necessary number of organisms that should be subsampled for biomonitoring includes considerations of taxonomic richness, level of identification used, acceptable error rates for impact detection, and magnitude of the effect size (Barbour and Gerritsen, 1996; Courtemanch, 1996; Vinson and Hawkins, 1996; Larsen and Herlihy, 1998; Cao and others, 2007). As with monitoring in many ecological systems, the full range of biological specimens collected typically is not analyzed. Given that total taxon richness is the most often used metric in State biomonitoring programs (see below), the inclusion and exclusion of taxa will influence the comparability of this measure among programs, and possibly even the comparability within a program over time, if the criteria for excluding certain taxa change over time or are different among projects.

Quality Assurance/Quality Control

The accurate identification of macroinvertebrates and the use of consistent methods for calculating metrics are of paramount importance in the interpretation of water quality both among programs and within a program over time (Ode and others, 2008; Haase and others, 2010; Cao and Hawkins, 2011). The importance of accurate macroinvertebrate identification is considered sufficiently critical for environmental studies that the SFS established a program to certify the taxonomic knowledge of individuals performing identifications of invertebrates (Society for Freshwater Science, http://www.nabstcp.com/). The SFS Taxonomic Certification

Program involves taking (and passing) tests on the identification of various groups of organisms. These tests are often specific to a regional fauna. Although, Rogers (2012) suggested that certification programs possibly may lead to inadequately reviewed taxonomic data, Stribling and others (2012) pointed out the need for proper QC procedures (i.e., proper review) whenever taxonomic data are used for bioassessments. Only a few programs indicated they presently required the SFS-based certification of those taxonomists identifying macroinvertebrates. To our knowledge, there are no equivalent programs for freshwater fishes or freshwater algae, which also are taxa used for biomonitoring in the U.S.

Just as taxonomic certification can lead to greater accuracy in macroinvertebrate identifications, the incorporation of other QC/QA techniques can lead to greater confidence in other aspects of bioassessment programs (Barbour and others, 2000; Yoder and Barbour, 2009). One-third of the programs (15/45) reported that they did not have a step in their laboratory protocol to determine the accuracy of the number of individuals sorted per taxon by having them recounted by a second taxonomist, which Stribling (2011) terms "percent difference in enumeration". This contrasts with an often cited recommended QC check, which generally has a criterion of an error of less than 10 percent of the initial count of organisms sorted (Barbour and others, 1999, Moulton and others, 2000). Enumerations are difficult for some groups (for example, colonial animals like sponges or bryozoans), and for organisms that fragment for reproduction or are mechanically broken apart (for example, naidid worms).

Retention of Samples

A decade ago, State programs collected between 13,000 and 15,000 samples per year (Carter and Resh, 2001), and that number is likely higher today. Consequently, the retention of all samples collected by a program is both space and cost prohibitive. Nevertheless, some taxonomists and environmental scientists have taken the position that unless sample identifications are verifiable, study results cannot be trusted; therefore, if voucher collections are not kept, a problem exists in confirming study results. Given the effort and expense in sorting and identifying macroinvertebrates from the many samples collected, the importance of properly curating voucher and reference collections seems obvious because: (1) it allows study results to be verified, (2) collections include a wealth of information on species distributions (Pyke and Ehrlich, 2010), and (3) they have the potential to increase the accuracy of determining regionally specific tolerance values (Whittier and Van Sickle, 2010) and species traits (Statzner and Bêche, 2010). With the rapid development of genetic tools (for example, Shaffer and others, 1998; Pilgrim and others, 2011; Sweeney and others, 2011) and the potential use of preserved specimens for food-web analyses (Sarakinos and others, 2002), these archived collections can be of great value in the future (Hajibabaei and others 2011; Lister and others, 2011).

Habitat Data Collected

The measurement of physical and chemical characteristics (often collectively known as habitat data) at a site in conjunction with the collection of benthic macroinvertebrate samples is an integral part of practically all biological-assessment programs (Barbour and others, 1999), and all State programs indicate they collect at least some habitat data at the same sites where they collect macroinvertebrate samples. There is, however, a great amount of variation in the per-site effort among States in collecting habitat data. Completion of visual habitat protocols can be rapid; however, completion of more intensive habitat protocols can require several people and many hours of costly field time (Fitzpatrick, 2001; Roper and others, 2010). Our data indicated that there is nearly a 3-fold difference in time spent by State programs using these two different protocol types. It is also probably fair to assume that the comparability of the habitat data derived from these two levels of effort differ substantially, as was found by Roper and others (2010) when comparing habitat protocols in the northwestern U.S. Although habitat data are used throughout the development of a biomonitoring program (for example, evaluating potential reference locations) and for specific bioassessments, many of these data are time consuming to collect; therefore, habitat data needs should be well-thought out, and the collected data should be thoroughly exploited (Kaufmann and others, 2009; Hughes and others, 2010). If these measures are used in identifying reference sites, than a standard set of variables and methods that span habitat-types should be developed.

Benthic Macroinvertebrate Data Preparation

The methods chosen for pre-treating data prior to analysis are a strict function of the data's attributes and the analyses to be performed (Downing 1979). Given that most programs appear to restrict their analyses to evaluating richness and percentage-based metrics, few data modifications (except relativizing as percentage composition per sample or site) were reported. This result contrasts with discussions that were common two to three decades ago that focused on the value of data pre-treatment techniques and ranged from discussions of which transformations were most appropriate to whether rare taxa should be eliminated before analyses were undertaken (Norris and Georges, 1993).

A diverse set of species traits have been in common use by European biological monitoring programs for more than two decades (Dolédec and Statzner, 2010; Menezes and others, 2010). However, the use of traits in the U.S. has been confined largely to the use of FFGs and tolerance values, with few exceptions (Richards and others, 1997; Merritt and others, 2002; Tullos and others, 2009). Recently, a large number of species traits have been developed for North American macroinvertebrates (Poff and others, 2006; Vieira and others, 2006) that potentially will be useful in biomonitoring in the U.S.

The use of FFGs in biomonitoring began with the incorporation of a filter-feeder metric by Plafkin and others (1989) and requires taxa to be categorized before data analysis. FFGs currently are evaluated as both richness and percentage-composition metrics (table 4). Resh and Jackson (1993) and others (Carter and others, 2006a) have pointed out that using data from the tables by Merritt and others (2008), as most programs reported, more reflects stomach contents than an insect's means of food acquisition as initially was intended by Cummins and Klug (1979); however, this may not limit the data's utility. The use of local expertise in categorizing FFGs, as reported by many State programs, may lead to more accurate assignments of FFGs at the local-level, but also may lead to greater among-program variability. Unfortunately, quantification of FFGs is more difficult than for many other species traits (for example, maximum body size, number of generations per year) (for example, Mihuc, 1997; Poff and others, 2006; Dolédec and Statzner, 2010; Resh and Rosenberg, 2010).

Determination of tolerance values typically has been based on sensitivity to oxygen depletion (i.e., through nutrient enrichment; Hilsenhoff, 1977; Bonada and others, 2006); however, the application of these values rarely has been restricted to evaluating this type of impact. Recently, Whittier and Van Sickle (2010) developed an assemblage tolerance index (ATI) that represents total tolerance. They conclude that the usefulness of their index could be improved by more rigorously and consistently collected chemical, physical, and biological data over time and space, an observation we also make relative to currently collected habitat data (see above).

The lack of geographic specificity, taxonomic resolution, and stressor specificity of tolerance values represent limitations in their use. However, our survey indicated that several States are developing tolerance values that are specific to their regions and for specific stressors, such as metals, acid mine drainage, and sediments. As with any indicator value, tolerance scores would be more intuitive to apply if they were on a linear scale where, for example, a tolerance value of 10 would represent an organism that has twice the tolerance as one with a score of 5 (Bonada and others, 2006).

Treatment of rare taxa is another aspect of data preparation that is troublesome (for example, Marchant, 2002; Van Sickle and others, 2007). Even though rare taxa frequently are encountered in both spatial and temporal benthic datasets (Resh and others, 2005), there are strong differences of opinion about what constitute rare taxa and what their role should be in biomonitoring. For example, one State program sorts large rare taxa during their sample processing, but only includes them in richness metrics (total taxon richness and EPT richness). Another program states that rare taxa are not considered in their calculation of O/E models. This latter situation may be common in many O/E-types of analyses (Carlisle and Meador, 2007) where the models are based primarily on taxa that have a high constancy (for example, percentage of samples or sites at which a taxon is collected). Additionally, Van Sickle and others (2007) showed that the exclusion of rare taxa often increases the sensitivity of O/E models. Other programs indicate that rare taxa confound the results of ordinations and, therefore, are eliminated prior to analysis (Marchant, 2002). Although rare taxa may add noise in some analyses, they may represent a variety of taxa, such as predaceous species, long-lived taxa, taxa near the limits of their habitat/physiological range, or possibly taxa just re-colonizing a previously impacted area. Thus, these rare taxa may be useful indicators of impact or recovery. Including or excluding rare taxa will influence estimates of richness at a site.

Choice of Metrics

Metrics represent the basis of most bioassessments in the U.S. Of the more than 100 metrics that were listed by the State programs, 11 of these metrics represent 50 percent of all metrics reported by the respondents (table 5). The choice of these 11 metrics may reflect their actual usefulness, attempts at uniformity with nearby State or Federal programs, or long-seated expectations that these metrics should "work". Approximately 66 percent of the metrics listed in table 4 and identified by the programs as having "high diagnostic value" (that is, were among the 10 most cited by a State) are used by only one state bioassessment program. A State may choose unique metrics because they elucidate a particularly uncommon local problem, but this level of "endemicity" seems high.

Measures of richness (for example, total, EPT, mayfly) are overwhelmingly the most popular type of metric used in State programs. Given the importance of richness measures to the State programs more consideration of the factors that have the potential to influence estimates of richness is necessary. Some of this factors include: the type of sampling procedures used (for example, to maximize richness or be representative of habitats examined), sorting procedures used in the laboratory (for example, number of individuals examined), the level of macroinvertebrate identifications, treatment of rare taxa, as well as other potential confounding factors.

Macroinvertebrate densities have long been known to be highly variable spatially and temporally (for example, Needham and Usinger, 1956; Resh, 1979), and only a few programs use density as a metric. Density may be a poor indicator of habitat quality (for example, Van Horne, 1983), and its accurate estimation depends on the procedures used for both sample collecting and processing; therefore, if density is used, as is suggested in the development of regionally-specific BCGs (Davies and Jackson, 2006), standardization among collection methods and laboratory processing is critical, as is providing a complete description of the methods used. Estimates of density are likely more reliable when fixed-area sampling is used, compared to a fixed effort as is used in fisheries research; however, only one program reports using a strictly fixed-area sampler (for example, Surber or Hess).

No programs reported using estimates of biomass or secondary production for bioassessments. Biomass estimates may be more useful than density estimates alone, but they are time consuming and often require the destruction of the organisms collected, which negates their future use for other purposes, including taxonomic validation. Measurements of secondary production, which are representative of energetics, have been reported to be one of the best estimates of ecosystem function available based on macroinvertebrates (Benke and Huryn, 2010), and they may be useful in biomonitoring as well (Bonada and others, 2006). However, accurate density and biomass estimates are critical for obtaining accurate estimates of secondary production, and the effort necessary is often extremely high.

Reference Sites or Conditions

The USEPA Science Advisory Board listed the "state of the science in defining ecoregions and reference areas" as one of the principal limitations in the use of biocriteria in water-quality studies (Science Advisory Board, 1993; p. 5). Since then, the advantages and disadvantages of using ecological regions, at least as the sole stratifying factor in water-quality studies based on macroinvertebrates, has been thoroughly evaluated (for example, Hawkins and others, 2000a and articles in this series). Moreover, even though there has been research on better understanding the concept of reference conditions (Stoddard and others, 2006), the process of adequately defining them has remained somewhat elusive (Whittier and others, 2007; Herlihy and others, 2008; Ode and others, 2008; Carter and others, 2009; Hawkins and others 2010b); therefore, the need to develop a systematic approach for the designation of reference conditions remains a critical task of biomonitoring research (Hawkins and others, 2010; Cao and Hawkins, 2011; Diamond and others, 2012).

Unlike chemical criteria that can be developed using bioassays, biocriteria typically are developed based on program- or study-specific reference sites. Our survey indicates that there appears to be a wide variety of methods used for establishing reference sites. Some State programs report that their reference sites are selected from a population of sites that have been identified using "probability-based methods" (Whittier and others, 2007), which we assume are based on those techniques used by USEPA programs (for example, Herlihy and others, 2008) or represent the reference sites selected by these large-scale programs implemented at the State-level (Ode and others, 2008). In general, programs report establishing reference sites by using a variety of methods, and often on a project-by-project basis. In any event, establishment of reference sites is a critical component of biomonitoring because they are the basis on which indices are developed and criteria are derived. An understanding of which specific factors are used and how these factors are used is critically important (Cao and Hawkins, 2011; Diamond and others, 2012).

State programs tend to use both landscape-level and local-scale variables when screening sites to use as reference sites. However, there seems to be little consensus from the results of our survey regarding which variables, regardless of scale, are the most useful to the States for this purpose. Earlier USEPA guidance indicated that the principal criteria should be restricted to large-scale variables, such as land use or land cover, population density, and ecophysiographic regions. It also implied that on-site physical and chemical variables should be avoided because bioassessments, in addition to evaluating the status of macroinvertebrates, often identify site-specific habitat and chemical impacts. USEPA surmised that using local-scale variables to identify reference sites could potentially lead to circularity in the assessment of these specific factors. However, studies by Herlihy and others (2008) and Ode and others (2008), as well as our results, indicate that it is currently not uncommon to consider variables representing both the landscape- and local-level when establishing reference sites.

Once a set of potential reference sites are chosen, State programs must decide whether each of the sites represents the reference condition (Whittier and others, 2007). Although there are a variety of factors used for this evaluation (for example, no upstream discharges that could influence site quality), the use of BPJ (i.e., using local knowledge and all available data and experience) was the most often cited approach in our survey. One potential problem of depending predominately on BPJ, however, is that it often involves a great deal of undocumented subjectivity. For example, some programs stated that reference sites in their states were chosen by their predecessors by using the BPJ approach, but they now lack detailed documentation regarding how these selections were made. Given the current use of BPJ for the establishment of reference sites by State programs and developing regionally specific BCGs (Davies and Jackson, 2006), it seems reasonable for this approach to be systematized and used as rigorously as possible, perhaps by instituting a standardization technique, such as the Delphi Method, or other approaches that quantify expert judgment (for example, Richy and others, 1985; Angermeier and others, 1991; Cao and Hawkins, 2011).

Regardless of the factors considered and methods used for establishing reference sites, States still seem to take a pragmatic approach to reference-site selection when appropriate. For example, in areas where an abundance of reference-quality sites exist, an important factor often cited is ease of access. Ease of access is almost always a deciding factor in bioassessment-site selection, and it has a strong influence on site selection in remote areas, many urban areas, and anywhere property rights influence access. There are many differences in the methods and criteria used by State programs for selecting reference sites. This variability will lead to differences in reference-site groups and, consequently, differences in test-site assessments (Cao and Hawkins, 2011, Diamond and others, 2012).

Statistical Calculations and Multivariate Analyses

Statistical analyses are a critical component of data interpretation in State programs. ANOVA, linear regression, and correlation are used in the metrics selection process, MMI development, and the formulation of biocriteria by many State programs. The use of statistics ranges from testing the effects of physical factors on individual metrics to determining whether sites meet their designated use. Historically, ANOVA [(and in its two sample analog, t-tests, along with many other more complicated ANOVA-based designs (Stewart-Oaten and others, 1986; Underwood, 1994)] has been used in upstream-downstream impact assessments, as well. It has been pointed out, however, that many of these studies are spatially confounded in the form in which they are normally applied (Hurlbert, 1984; Underwood, 1997).

Several (22) States have development of O/E models on their "to do" list. O/E is a multivariate approach for developing an index used for monitoring water quality that was initially developed in the UK as RIVPACs and now is used widely in Australia, Canada, and by some agencies in the U.S. Traditionally, the USEPA emphasized MMI development, which is reflected in the importance of metric evaluations and MMI development at the State level. Currently, O/E approaches are viewed as complementary to MMIs (Hawkins, 2006; Norris and Barbour, 2009). Carter and others (2006a) present a flow diagram describing the steps in the use of O/E (RIVPACS) models and the difference between O/E and multimetric approaches. The Website (http://cnr.usu.edu/wmc/) is a useful primer on O/E model development.

Data Storage

All programs store their data in electronic format and, likewise, all have established databases. Not all programs post their data to the Web. However, posting their macroinvertebrate data would not only lead to a far more transparent process of the assessments undertaken by the States, but would likely increase public awareness of biological monitoring in general. We believe that the more the public knows about the process of a program, the higher the probability it will be supported.

Last, accurate nomenclature greatly aids the long-term usefulness of macroinvertebrate data. However, printed sources are often out of date soon after they appear. An electronically based system (for example, http://www.itis.gov/) can be updated quickly, but it needs to have broad technical and financial support to remain current.

Conclusions

There are 5 key points that we feel have emerged from our survey that are deserving of further attention. First, based on our analyses and on the importance of effectively approximating the reference condition and identifying reference sites for subsequently assessing impaired sites, we strongly believe that a national-level need exists for establishing a set of common practices for selecting reference sites, however difficult this task may be (Whittier and others, 2007). If unique classifications (Hawkins and others, 2000a), such as ecoregions, are used, then at a minimum, further partitioning is necessary (McCarron and Frydenborg, 1997; Ode and others, 2008). Conversely, since Hawkins and Vinson (2000) pointed out the limitations of classifications in general when representing the continuous relationship that exists between macroinvertebrates and their environment, a more appropriate approach will likely involve modeling these influences by using methods similar to an O/E approach (Wright and others, 2000), which more effectively partitions these influences. The results of our survey indicate that many States already evaluate both large-scale geographic criteria and local-scale physicochemical variables when selecting reference sites. Additionally, at least some programs also evaluate macroinvertebrate species composition in this process; therefore, the transition to a national (or regional) approach that systematically identifies and partitions reference conditions seems possible. Regardless of the method developed, however, it must take into account specific within-State needs, as well as lead to greater regional and (or) national consistency. Development of a nationally consistent technique for identifying reference conditions would have the potential not only to systematize this important aspect of biomonitoring, but to make the process potentially more objective than it has been in the past.

A second priority would be to increase the comparability among state programs in how richness is determined. Issues surrounding the estimation of species richness have a long history in benthic biology, and studies have repeatedly demonstrated that richness estimates are extremely method-specific (Barbour and Gerritsen, 1996; Courtemanch, 1996; Vinson and Hawkins, 1996; Larsen and Herlihy, 1998). Given the priority placed on measures of richness as a metric used by the States, any assessment of regional or national scope must assume that richness estimates obtained from the same site will be similar if determined simultaneously by two separate programs (U.S. Environmental Protection Agency, 2003). The only solution to establishing comparable estimates of richness is the application of more uniform techniques among programs in terms of sample collection and processing, including identification procedures, given the dependency of estimates of richness on these factors (Cao and Hawkins, 2011). Any errors related to the identification of macroinvertebrates (Haase and others, 2010) may, in time, become a moot point with the development of a national DNA-barcode library (Baird and others, 2011) and the increased application of DNA techniques in water-quality studies (Sweeney and others, 2011). Increased uniformity among programs also will involve increased uniformity in the techniques used by contractors because they currently process samples from more than 50 percent of the State programs.

As a third priority, because metrics are an important component of many State programs, the testing and documentation of metrics is a critical need in benthic macroinvertebrate bioassessments. Some of the more than 100 metrics considered useful by one or more of the State programs (table 4) may be worth considering by other bioassessment programs. It seems especially important that metrics should be chosen not only based on correlative information and their ability to distinguish impaired from unimpaired sites locally, but also on documented theory and known mechanistic responses to known stressor gradients (McCarron and Frydenborg, 1997; Bonada and others, 2006; Davies and Jackson, 2006). In addition, the use of multiple lines of evidence techniques can be used to establish the value and validity of particular metrics in evaluating different impacts (Norris and others, 2005, 2008). Documentation of these attributes for widely used metrics should be a national priority and would lead to more defensible and geographically generalizable assessments.

Fourth, the lack of information provided by the States on the design of point-source studies likely is related to the shift during the last few decades from effluent-base monitoring to ambient monitoring (National Research Center, 2001 but see U.S. Environmental Protection Agency, 2010). Nevertheless, the need for appropriately designed point-source studies still exists. Many of the programs reported that they did not perceive sites as replicates; however, sites are always considered replicates (Hawkins and others, 2000b) when they are used to establish regional reference conditions for the development and analysis of nonpoint-source studies (that is, ambient monitoring). Because some programs do not consider sites as replicates, it is possible that point-source studies undertaken by these programs are pseudoreplicated as a result of within-site "replication", which greatly compromises their validity (Hurlbert, 1984). Based on our survey results, it is probable that state-wide assessments have developed enough data from ambient monitoring programs to design point-source studies that are replicated at an appropriate scale (i.e., at the level of the site or larger), using replicated reference sites as controls (Hawkins and others, 2010b).

Finally, the biological data gathered by State programs, when systematically and consistently collected and curated, could prove critical to understanding the environmental changes anticipated in the coming decades (Lister and others, 2011). These historical collections are extremely valuable. For example, collections made at biological stations and field-research institutions have served as an important basis for examining faunal changes over time (Shaffer and others, 1998; Casas-Marce and others, 2012), and many examples are known for benthic macroinvertebrates (for example, Resh and Unzicker, 1975; Hall and Ide, 1987; Dewalt and others, 2005). Moreover, new techniques have recently appeared and are being further developed that can significantly increase the information content and usefulness of species collected for bioassessments (for example, Pilgram and others, 2011; Sweeney and others, 2011). However, to be successful in this effort, funding must be provided for the proper curation of this valuable and irreplaceable national resource.

In conclusion, the results of our survey point out some of the analytical factors that vary among State monitoring programs. The effects of this variability need to be evaluated if data comparability among State programs is a priority (U.S. Environmental Protection Agency, 2003; Roper and others, 2010). State data that were generated by using identical techniques and then properly combined would be well-suited for determining ambient water quality both regionally and nationally (Cao and Hawkins, 2011), especially when supported by a uniformly applied method evaluation technique and impairment framework (Davies and Jackson, 2006; Yoder and Barbour, 2009; Diamond and others, 2012).

Water-quality monitoring in the U.S. continues to be a partnership between the individual States and USEPA, as defined by the CWA. This relationship has been complementary and has resulted in many successful programs during the past several decades. It is clear that future successes in biomonitoring are dependent on adequate funding (U. S. Government Accounting Office, 2009) as biomonitoring responsibilities will increase as a result of increasing population and natural (i.e., climate change) pressures on our aquatic systems.

Acknowledgments

We thank the State biologists who graciously gave their time to answer our long and often complicated survey, and respond to our repeated telephone inquiries. Their efforts on this survey reflect their interests in seeing that biomonitoring advances at both the State and Federal level. We also thank Phil Kaufmann and Jainni Xin for their assistance, and Barbara Eikenberry and Steve Fend for their helpful comments.

References

Angermeier, P.L., Naves, R.J., and Nielsen, L.A., 1991, Assessing stream values—Perspectives of aquatic resource professionals: North American Journal of Fishery Management, v. 11, p. 1–10.

Baird, D.J., Pascoe, T.J., Zhou, X., and Hajibabaei, M., 2011, Building freshwater macroinvertebrate DNA-barcode libraries from reference collection material—Formalin preservation vs specimen age: Journal of the North American Benthological Society, v. 30, p. 125–130.

Barbour, M.T., and Gerritsen, J., 1996, Subsampling of benthic samples—A defense of the fixed count method: Journal of the North American Benthological Society, v. 15, p. 386–391.

Barbour, M.T., Gerritsen, J., Snyder, B.D., and Stribling, J.B., 1999, Rapid bioassessment protocols for use in streams and wadeable rivers: periphyton, benthic macroinvertebrates and fish: Office of Water, U.S. Environmental Protection Agency EPA 841-B-99-002.

Barbour, M.T., Swietlik, W.F., Jackson, S.K., Courtemanch, D.L., Davies, S.P., and Yoder, C.O., 2000, Measuring the attainment of biological integrity in the USA—A critical element of ecological integrity: Hydrobiologia, v. 422/423, p. 453–464.

Barbour, M.T., and Yoder, C.O., 2000, The multimetric approach to bioassessment, as used in the United States of America, *in* Wright, J.F., Sutcliffe, D.W., and Furse, M.T., eds., Assessing the biological quality of fresh waters—RIVPACS and other techniques: Ambleside, Cumbria, UK, Freshwater Biological Association, p. 281–292.

Benke, A.C., and Huryn, A.D., 2010, Benthic invertebrate production—Facilitating answers to ecological riddles in freshwater ecosystems: Journal of the North American Benthological Society, v. 29, no. 1, p. 264–285.

Bonada, N., Prat, N., Resh, V., and Statzner, B., 2006, Developments in aquatic insect biomonitoring—A comparative analysis of recent approaches: Annual Review of Entomology, v. 51, p. 495–524.

Cao, Y., Hawkins, C., Larsen, D., and VanSickle, J., 2007, Effects of sample standardization on mean species detectabilities and estimates of relative differences in species richness among assemblages: American Naturalist, v. 170, no. 3, p. 381–395.

Cao, Y., and Hawkins, C.P., 2011, The comparability of bioassessments—Review of conceptual and methodological issues: Journal of the North American Benthological Society, v. 30, p. 680–701.

Carlisle, D.M., and Meador, M.R., 2007, A biological assessment of streams in the eastern United States using a predictive model for macroinvertebrate assemblages: JAWRA Journal of the American Water Resources Association, v. 43, no. 5, p. 1194–1207.

Carter, J.L., Purcell, A.H., Fend, S.V., and Resh, V.H., 2009, Development of a local-scale urban assessment method using benthic macroinvertebrates—An example from the Santa Clara Basin, California: Journal of the North American Benthological Society, v. 28, p. 1007–1021.

Carter, J.L., and Resh, V.H., 2001, After site selection and before data analysis—Sampling, sorting, and laboratory procedures used in stream benthic macroinvertebrate monitoring programs by USA state agencies: Journal North American Benthological Society, v. 20, no. 4, p. 658–682.

Carter, J.L., Resh, V.H., Hanniford, M.J., and Myers, M.J., 2006a, Macroinvertebrates as biotic indicators of environmental quality, *in* Hauer, F.R., and Lamberti, G.A., eds., Methods in stream ecology (2d ed.): San Diego, Calif., Academic Press, p. 805–833.

Carter, J.L., Resh, V.H., Rosenberg, D.M., and Reynoldson, T.B., 2006b, Biomonitoring in North American rivers—A comparison of methods used for benthic macroinvertebrates in Canada and the United States, *in* Ziglio, G., Siligardi, M., and Flaim, G., eds., Biological monitoring of rivers—Applications and perspectives: N.Y., John Wiley & Sons, p. 203–228.

Casas-Marce, M., Revilla, E., Fernandes, M., Rodriguez, A., Delibes, M., and Godoy, J.A., 2012, The value of hidden scientific resources—Preserved animal specimens from private collections and small museums: BioScience, v. 62, no. 12, p. 1077–1082.

Courtemanch, D.L., 1996, Commentary on the subsampling procedures used for rapid bioassessments: Journal of the North American Benthological Society, v. 15, p. 381–385.

Cummins, K.W., and Klug, M.J., 1979, Feeding ecology of stream invertebrates: Annual Review of Ecology and Systematics, v. 10, p. 147–172.

Davies, S.P., and Jackson, S.K., 2006, The biological condition gradient—A descriptive model for interpreting change in aquatic ecosystems: Ecological Applications, v. 16, no. 4, p. 1251-1266.

DeWalt, R.E., Favret, C., and Webb, D.W., 2005, Just how imperiled are aquatic insects—A case study of stoneflies (Plecoptera) in Illinois: Annual Entomological Society of America, v. 98, p. 941–950.

Diamond, J., Stribling, J., Huff, L., and Gilliam, J., 2012, An approach for determining bioassessment performance and comparability: Environmental Monitoring and Assessment, v. 184, no. 4, p. 2247–2260.

Dolédec, S., and Statzner, B., 2010, Responses of freshwater biota to human disturbances— Contribution of J-NABS to developments in ecological integrity assessments: Journal of the North American Benthological Society, v. 29, no. 1, p. 286–311.

Downes, B.J., Barmuta, L.A., Fairweather, P.G., Faith, D.P., Keough, M.J., Lake, P.S., Mapstone, B.D., and Quinn, G.P., 2002, Monitoring ecological impacts: concepts and practice in flowing waters: United Kingdom, Cambridge University Press, 434 p.

Downing, J.A., 1979, Aggregation, transformation and the design of benthos sampling programs: Journal of the Fisheries Board of Canada, v. 36, p. 1454–1463.

EDAS2, 2013, Environmental Data Analysis System. Accessed June 6, 2013, at http://www.edas2.com/.

Fitzpatrick, F.A., 2001, A comparison of multi-disciplinary methods for measuring physical conditions of streams, in Dorava, J.B., Montgomery, D.R., Palcsak, B., and Fitzpatrick, F.A., eds., Geomorphic processes and riverine habitat: Washington, D.C., American Geophysical Union Monograph, p. 7–18.

Green, R.H., 1979, Sampling design and statistical methods for environmental biologists: N.Y., John Wiley, 272 p.

Haase, P., Pauls, S.U., Schindehütte, K., and Sundermann, A., 2010, First audit of macroinvertebrate samples from an EU water framework directive monitoring program— Human error greatly lowers precision of assessment results: Journal of the North American Benthological Society, v. 29, no. 4, p. 1279–1291.

Hajibabaei, M., Shokralla, S., Zhou, X., Singer, G.A.C., and Baird, D.J., 2011, Environmental barcoding—A next-generation sequencing approach for biomonitoring applications using river benthos: PLoS ONE, v. 6, no. 4, p. e17497.

Hall, R.J., and Ide, F.R., 1987, Evidence of acidification effects on stream insect communities in central Ontario between 1937 and 1985: Canadian Journal of Fisheries and Aquatic Sciences, v. 44, p. 1652–1657.

Hawkins, C.P., 2006, Quantifying biological integrity by taxonomic completeness—Its utility in regional and global assessments: Ecological Applications, v. 16, p. 1277–1294.

Hawkins, C.P., Norris, R.H., Gerritsen, J., Hughes, R.M., Jackson, S.K., Johnson, R.K., and Stevenson, R.J., 2000a, Evaluation of the use of landscape classifications for the prediction of freshwater biota—Synthesis and recommendations: Journal of the North American Benthological Society, v. 19, no. 3, p. 541–556.

Hawkins, C.P., Norris, R.H., Hogue, J.N., and Feminella, J.W., 2000b, Development and evaluation of predictive models for measuring the biological integrity of streams: Ecological Applications, v. 10, no. 5, p. 1456–1477.

Hawkins, C.P., Olson, J.R., and Hill, R.A., 2010, The reference condition—Predicting benchmarks for ecological and water-quality assessments: Journal of the North American Benthological Society, v. 29, no. 1, p. 312–343.

Hawkins, C.P., and Vinson, M.R., 2000, Weak correspondence between landscape classifications and stream invertebrate assemblages—Implications for bioassessment: Journal of the North American Benthological Society, v. 19, no. 3, p. 501–517.

The H. John Heinz III Center for Science Economics and the Environment, 2008, Highlights—The state of the nation's ecosystems 2008—Measuring the lands, waters, and living resources of the United States: The Heinz Center, 44 p.

Herlihy, A.T., Paulsen, S.G., Sickle, J.V., Stoddard, J.L., Hawkins, C.P., and Yuan, L.L., 2008, Striving for consistency in a national assessment: the challenges of applying a reference-condition approach at a continental scale: Journal of the North American Benthological Society, v. 27, no. 4, p. 860–877.

Hilsenhoff, W.L., 1977, Use of arthropods to evaluate water quality of streams: Wisconsin Department of Natural Resources Technical Bulletin, v. 100, p. 1-15.

Hilsenhoff, W.L., 1987, An improved biotic index of organic stream pollution: Great Lakes Entomologist, v. 20, p. 31–39.

Hilsenhoff, W.L., 1988, Rapid field assessment of organic pollution with a family-level biotic index: Journal of the North American Benthological Society, v. 7, p. 65–68.

Hilsenhoff, W.L., 1998, A modification of the biotic index of organic stream pollution to remedy problems and permit its use throughout the year: Great Lakes Entomologist, v. 31, p. 1–12.

Hornberger, M.I., Luoma, S.N., Johnson, M.L., and Holyoa, M., 2009, Influence of remediation in a mine-impacted river: metal trends over large spatial and temporal scales: Ecological Applications, v. 19, p. 1522–1535.

Hughes, R.M., Herlihy, A.T., and Kaufmann, P.R., 2010, An evaluation of qualitative indexes of physical habitat applied to agricultural streams in ten U.S. states: Journal of the American Water Resources Association, v. 46, no. 4, p. 792–806.

ITIS, 2013, Integrated Taxonomic Information System, accessed June 6, 2013, at http://www.itis.gov/

Hurlbert, S.H., 1984, Pseudoreplication and the design of ecological field experiments: Ecological Monographs, v. 54, p. 187–211.

Kaufmann, P.R., Larsen, D.P., and Faustini, J.M., 2009, Bed stability and sedimentation associated with human disturbances in Pacific Northwest streams: Journal of the American Water Resources Association, v. 45, p. 434–459.

Kenney, M.A., Sutton-Grier, A.E., Smith, R.F., and Gresens, S.E., 2009, Benthic macroinvertebrates as indicators of water quality—The intersection of science and policy: Terrestrial Arthropod Reviews, v. 2, p. 99–128.

Kondolf, G.M., 1995, Five elements for effective evaluation of stream restoration: Restoration Ecology, v. 3, p. 133–136.

Larsen, D.P., and Herlihy, A.T., 1998, The dilemma of sampling streams for macroinvertebrate richness: Journal of the North American Benthological Society, v. 17, p. 359–365.

Lenat, D.R., 1993, A Biotic Index for the southeastern United States—Derivation and list of tolerance values, with criteria for assigning water-quality ratings: Journal of the North American Benthological Society, v. 12, no. 3, p. 279–290.

Lister, A.M., Brooks, S.J., Fenberg, P.B., Glover, A.G., James, K.E., Michael, K.G.E., Okamura, B., Spencer, M., Stewart, J.R., Todd, J.A., Valsami-Jones, E., and Yong, J., 2011, Natural history collections as sources of long-term datasets: Trends in Ecology & Evolution, v. 26, no. 4, p. 153–154.

Marchant, R., 2002, Do rare species have any place in multivariate analysis for bioassessment?: Journal- North American Benthological Society, v. 21, no. 2, p. 311–313.

McCarron, E., and Frydenborg, R., 1997, The Florida bioassessment program: an agent of change: Human and Ecological Risk Assessment, v. 3, p. 967–977.

Menezes, S., Baird, D.J., and Soares, A.M.V.M., 2010, Beyond taxonomy—A review of macroinvertebrate trait-based community descriptors as tools for freshwater biomonitoring: Journal of Applied Ecology, v. 47, no. 4, p. 711–719.

Merritt, R., Cummins, K., Berg, M., Novak, J., Higgins, M., Wessell, K., and Lessard, J., 2002, Development and application of a macroinvertebrate functional-group approach in the bioassessment of remnant river oxbows in southwest Florida: Journal of the North American Benthological Society, v. 21, no. 2, p. 290–310.

Merritt, R.W., Cummins, K.W., and Berg, M.B., eds., 2008, An introduction to the aquatic insects of North America (4th ed.): Dubuque, Iowa, Kendall/Hunt Publishing Co, 1158 p.

Mihuc, T.B., 1997, The functional trophic role of lotic primary consumers—Generalist versus specialist strategies: Freshwater Biology, v. 37, no. 2, p. 455–462.

Moulton II, S.R., Carter, J.L., Grotheer, S.A., Cuffney, T.F., and Short, T.M., 2000, Methods of analysis by the U.S. Geological Survey National Water Quality Laboratory—Processing, taxonomy, and quality control of benthic macroinvertebrate samples: Colo. U.S. Geological Survey Open-File Report 00-212.

Needham, P.R., and Usinger, R.L., 1956, Variability in the macrofauna of a single riffle in Prosser Creek, California, as indicated by the Surber sampler: Hilgardia, v. 24, p. 383–409.

NEMI, 2013, National Environmental Methods Index, accessed June 6, 2013, at https://www.nemi.gov/apex/f?p=237:1:4496253571008062.

Norris, R.H., and Barbour, M.T., 2009, Bioassessment of aquatic ecosystems, in Likens, G.E., ed., Encyclopedia of inland waters.: Oxford, Elsevier, p. 21–28.

Norris, R.H., and Georges, A., 1993, Analysis and interpretation of benthic macroinvertebrate surveys, in Rosenberg, D.M., and Resh, V.H., eds., Freshwater biomonitoring and benthic macroinvertebrates: N.Y., Chapman & Hall, p. 234–286.

Norris, R.H., Liston, P., Mugodo, J., Nichols, S., Quinn, G., Cottingham, P., Metzeling, L., Perriss, S., Robinson, D., Tiller, D., and Wilson, G., 2005, Multiple lines and levels of evidence for detecting ecological responses to management intervention, in Rutherfurd, I.D., Wiszniewski, I., Askey-Doran, M.J., and Glazik, R., eds., Proceedings of the 4th Australian Stream Management Conference—Linking rivers to landscapes: Hobar, Tasmania, Australia, Department of Primary Industries, Water and Environment, p. 456–463.

Norris, R.H., Nichols, S., Ransom, G., Webb, A., Stewardson, M., Liston, P., and Mugodo, J., 2008, Causal criteria analysis methods manual: a systematic approach to evaluate causality in environmental science: Canberra, eWater Cooperative Research Centre.

NRC (National Research Council), 2001, Assessing the TMDL approach to water quality management, committee to assess the scientific basis of the total maximum daily load approach to pollution reduction: Washington, D.C., National Academy Press.

Ode, P.R., Hawkins, C.P., and Mazor, R.D., 2008, Comparability of biological assessments derived from predictive models and multimetric indices of increasing geographic scope: Journal of the North American Benthological Society, v. 27, no. 4, p. 967–985.

Omernik, J.M., 1987, Map supplement: ecoregions of the conterminous United States: Annals of the Association of American Geographers, v. 77, p. 118–125.

ORACLE, Oracle Corp. Redwood Shores, Calif.

Pilgrim, E.M., Jackson, S.A., Swenson, S., Turcsanyi, I., Friedman, E., Weigt, L., and Bagley, M.J., 2011, Incorporation of DNA barcoding into a large-scale biomonitoring program— Opportunities and pitfalls: Journal of the North American Benthological Society, v. 30, no. 1, p. 217–231.

Plafkin, J.L., Barbour, M.T., Porter, K.D., Gross, S.K., and Hughes, R.M., 1989, Rapid bioassessment protocols for use in streams and rivers—Benthic macroinvertebrates and fish: Washington, D.C., U.S. Environmental Protection Agency, Report No. 444/4-89-001.

Poff, N., Olden, J., Vieira, N., Finn, D., Simmons, M., and Kondratieff, B., 2006, Functional trait niches of North American lotic insects—Traits-based ecological applications in light of phylogenetic relationships: Journal- North American Benthological Society, v. 25, no. 4, p. 730–755.

Purcell, A.H., Friedrich, C., and Resh, V.H., 2002, An assessment of a small, urban stream restoration project in Northern California: Restoration Ecology, v. 10, p. 685–694.

Pyke, G.H., and Ehrlich, P.R., 2010, Biological collections and ecological/environmental research—A review, some observations and a look to the future: Biological Reviews, v. 85, no. 2, p. 247–266.

Resh, V.H., 1979, Sampling variability and life history features—Basic considerations in the design of aquatic insect studies: Journal of the Fisheries Board of Canada, v. 36, p. 290–311.

Resh, V.H., Bêche, L.A., and McElravy, E.P., 2005, How common are rare taxa in long-term benthic macroinvertebrate surveys?: Journal- North American Benthological Society, v. 24, no. 4, p. 976–989.

Resh, V.H., and Jackson, J.K., 1993, Rapid assessment approaches to biomonitoring using benthic macroinvertebrates, in Rosenberg, D.M., and Resh, V.H., eds., Freshwater biomonitoring and benthic macroinvertebrates: N.Y., Chapman & Hall, p. 195–223.

Resh, V.H., and McElravy, E.P., 1993, Contemporary quantitative approaches to biomonitoring using benthic macroinvertebrates, in Rosenberg, D.M., and Resh, V.H., eds., Freshwater biomonitoring and benthic macroinvertebrates: N.Y., Chapman & Hall, p. 159–194.

Resh, V.H., and Rosenberg, D.M., 2010, Recent trends in life-history research on benthic macroinvertebrates: Journal of the North American Benthological Society, v. 29, no. 1, p. 207–219.

Resh, V.H., and Unzicker, J.D., 1975, Water quality monitoring and aquatic organisms—The importance of species identification: Water Quality Monitoring, v. 47, p. 9–19.

Richards, C., Haro, R.J., Johnson, L.B., and Host, G.E., 1997, Catchment and reach-scale properties as indicators of macroinvertebrate species traits: Freshwater Biology, v. 37, p. 219–230.

Richy, J.S., Mar, B.W., and Horner, R.R., 1985, Delphi technique in environmental assessment I—Implementation and effectiveness: Journal of Environmental Management, v. 21, p. 135–146.

Rogers, D.C., 2012, Taxonomic certification versus the scientific methods: Zootaxa, v. 3257, no. 66–68.

Roper, B.B., Buffington, J.M., Bennett, S., Lanigan, S.H., Archer, E., Downie, S.T., Faustini, J., Hillman, T.W., Hubler, S., Jones, K., Jordan, C., Kaufmann, P.R., Merritt, G., Moyer, C., and Pleus, A., 2010, A comparison of the performance and compatibility of protocols used by seven monitoring groups to measure stream habitat in the Pacific Northwest: North American Journal of Fisheries Management, v. 30, no. 2, p. 565–587.

Science Advisory Board, 1993, An SAB report—Evaluation of draft technical guidance on biological criteria for streams and small rivers: Washington, D.C., Biological Criteria Subcommittee of the Ecological Processes and Effects Committee, EPA-SAB-EPEC-94-003.

Sarakinos, H.C., Johnson, M.L., and Zanden, M.J.V., 2002, A synthesis of tissue-preservation effects on carbon and nitrogen stable isotope signatures: Canadian Journal of Zoology, v. 80, no. 2, p. 381.

Shaffer, H.B., Fisher, R.N., and Davidson, C., 1998, The role of natural history collections in documenting species declines: Trends in Ecology and Evolution, v. 13, p. 27–30.

Shapiro, M.H., Holdsworth, S.M., and Paulsen, S.G., 2008, The need to assess the condition of aquatic resources in the U.S.: Journal of the North American Benthological Society, v. 27, no. 4, p. 808–811.

Society for Freshwater Science, 2013, Taxonomic Certification Programme, accessed June 6, 2013, at http://www.nabstcp.com/.

StatSoft, Inc., 2012, STATISTICA (data analysis software system): version 9. www.statsoft.com

Statzner, B., and Bêche, L.A., 2010, Can biological invertebrate traits resolve effects of multiple stressors on running water ecosystems?: Freshwater Biology, v. 55, p. 80–119.

Stewart-Oaten, A., Murdoch, W.W., and Parker, K.R., 1986, Environmental impact assessment—Pseudo-replication in time?: Ecology, v. 67, p. 929–940.

Stoddard, J., Larsen, D., Hawkins, C., Johnson, R., and Norris, R., 2006, Setting expectations for the ecological condition of streams: the concept of reference condition: Ecological Applications, v. 16, no. 4, p. 1267–1276.

Stribling, J.B., 2011, Partitioning error sources for quality control and comparability analysis in biological monitoring and assessment, in Elding, A.B., ed., Modern approaches to quality control. In Tech Open Access Publisher, p. 59–84., accessed (June 5m 2013), at http://www.intechopen.com/articles/show/title/partitioning-error-sources-for-quality-control-and-comparability-analysis-in-biological-monitoring-a.

Stribling, J.B., Sweeney, B.W., Morse, J.C., Corkum, G., Lester, G., Miller, S.W., Mitchell, R., Poulton, B., Strachan, S., and Wetzel, M.A., 2012, Taxonomic certification versus the scientific method—A rebuttal of Rogers (2012): Zootaxa, v. 3359, p. 65–68.

Sweeney, B.W., Battle, J.M., Jackson, J.K., and Dapkey, T., 2011, Can DNA barcodes of stream macroinvertebrates improve descriptions of community structure and water quality?: Journal of the North American Benthological Society, v. 30, no. 1, p. 195–216.

Tullos, D.D., Penrose, D.L., Jennings, G.D., and Cope, W.G., 2009, Analysis of functional traits in reconfigured channels: implications for the bioassessment and disturbance of river restoration: Journal of the North American Benthological Society, v. 28, no. 1, p. 80–92.

Underwood, A.J., 1994, On beyond BACI—Sampling designs that might reliably detect environmental disturbance: Ecological Applications, v. 4, p. 3–15.

Underwood, A.J., 1997, Experiments in ecology—Their logical design and interpretation using analysis of variance: Cambridge, UK, Cambridge University Press, 524 p.

U.S. Environmental Protection Agency, 1996, Summary of state biological assessment programs for streams and wadeable rivers: EPA 230-R-96-007, 168 p.

U.S. Environmental Protection Agency, 2002, Summary of biological assessment programs and biocriteria development for states, tribes, territories, and interstate commissions: streams and wadeable rivers: EPA 822-R-02-048, 401 p.

U.S. Environmental Protection Agency, 2003, Elements of a state water monitoring and assessment program: Office of Wetlands, Oceans and Watershed, U.S. Environmental Protection Agency EPA 841-B-03-003, 24 p.

U.S. Environmental Protection Agency, 2010, MS4 improvement guide: Office of Water, U.S. Environmental Protection Agency, EPA 833-R-10-001.

U.S. Environmental Protection Agency, 2012, STORET, accessed June 6, 2013, at http://www.epa.gov/storet/.

U.S. Government Accounting Office, 1989, Federal Water Pollution Control Act (33 U. S. C. 1251 et seq.) as amended by a P. L. 92-500.

U.S. Government Accounting Office, 2009, Clean Water Act—Longstanding issues impact EPAs and States enforcement efforts. GAO-10-165T.

Van Horne, B., 1983, Density as a misleading indicator of habitat quality: Journal of Wildlife Management, v. 47, p. 893–901.

Van Sickle, J., Larsen, D.P., and Hawkins, C.P., 2007, Exclusion of rare taxa affects performance of the O/E index in bioassessments: Journal of the North American Benthological Society, v. 26, p. 319–331.

Vieira, N.K.M., Poff, N.L., Carlisle, D.M., Moulton Ii, S.R., Koshi, M.L., and Kondratieff, B.C., 2006, A database of lotic invertebrate traits for North America: U.S. Geological Survey Data Series 187.

Vinson, M.R., and Hawkins, C.P., 1996, Effects of sampling area and subsampling procedure on comparisons of taxa richness among streams: Journal of the North American Benthological Society, v. 15, p. 392–399.

Voshell, J.R., Layton, R.J., and Hiner, S.W., 1989, Field techniques for determining the effects of toxic substances on benthic macroinvertebrates in rocky-bottom streams, in Cowgill, U.M., and Williams, L.R., eds., Aquatic toxicology and hazard assessment: Philadelphia, Pa., [American Society for Testing and Materials,] volume 12, ASTM Special Technical Publication 1027, 427 p.

Western Center for Monitoring and Assessment of Freshwater Ecosystems, 2013, Utah State University, accessed June 6, 2013 at http://cnr.usu.edu/wmc/.

Whittier, T., Stoddard, J., Larsen, D., and Herlihy, A., 2007, Selecting reference sites for stream biological assessments—Best professional judgement or objective criteria: Journal- North American Benthological Society, v. 26, no. 2, p. 349–360.

Whittier, T.R., and Van Sickle, J., 2010, Macroinvertebrate tolerance values and an assemblage tolerance index (ATI) for western USA streams and rivers: Journal of the North American Benthological Society, v. 29, no. 3, p. 852–866.

Winterbourn, M.J., 1985, Sampling stream invertebrates, in Pridmore, R.D., and Cooper, A.B., eds., Biological monitoring in freshwaters: proceedings of a seminar, Hamilton, November 21-23, 1984, Part 2, Water and soil miscellaneous publication no. 83: Wellington, New Zealand, National Water and Soil Conservation Authority, p. 241–258.

Wright, J.F., Sutcliffe, D.W., and Furse, M.T., eds., 2000, Assessing the biological quality of fresh water—RIVPACS and other techniques: Ambleside, UK, Freshwater Biological Association, 373 p.

Yoder, C.O., and Barbour, M.T., 2009, Critical technical elements of state bioassessment programs—A process to evaluate program rigor and comparability: Environmental Monitoring and Assessment, v. 150, p. 31–42.

Table 1. Priority listing of the purposes reported by State monitoring programs.

[Bold values represent the frequency that each purpose was identified. Non-bold values represent the frequencies weighted by the priority given by the State programs. See the Methods for section an explanation of weighting]

Priority ranking	State regulations		Biotic Index development		Research		Federal regulations		Local regulations		Observed/Expected development	
	Count	Rank	Count	Rank	Count	Rank	Count	Rank	Count	Rank	Count	Rank
1	27	216.0	8	64.0	1	8.0	7	56.0	1	8.0	2	16.0
2	13	45.5	13	45.5	3	10.5	9	31.5	3	10.5	3	10.5
3	5	10.0	12	24.0	6	12.0	8	16.0	5	10.0	3	6.0
4	1	11.3	8	10.0	6	7.5	4	5.0	3	3.8	3	3.8
5			1	0.8	7	5.6	1	0.8	8	6.4	4	3.2
6			1	1.0	8	4.0			4	2.0	1	0.5
7					2	0.6					5	1.4
8											1	0.1
Total	46	273	43	145	33	48	29	109	24	41	22	42

29

Table 2. Frequency that factors are used for stratifying areas for the determination of reference sites.

[Factors are ordered by the total frequency of use]

Factor	Primary choice	Second-fourth choice	Total
Ecoregion	22	7	29
Area	3	11	14
Land cover	1	10	11
Elevation	0	10	10
Stream gradient	0	9	9
Physiographic region	4	1	5
Stream order	0	5	5
Geology	0	5	5
Water chemistry	0	4	4
Major basin	2	1	3
Latitude/longitude	1	2	3
Road density	1	2	3
Flow	0	3	3
Temperature	0	3	3
Human disturbance	0	3	3
Best Professional Judgment	1	1	2
Substratum	0	2	2
Political boundary	1	0	1
Tiered aquatic life	1	0	1
Climate	1	0	1
Riparian	0	1	1
Season	0	1	1
Sampling method	0	1	1
Existing data	0	1	1
Julian day	0	1	1
Total	38	84	122

Table 3. Number of organisms selected for fixed-counting sorting procedures reported by Carter and Resh (2001) and for this survey (2010).

Fixed count	2010	2001	Difference between 2010 and 2001
≤100	11	22	-11
101–199	3	2	+1
200	6	3	+3
300	12	12	0
500	9	4	+5
Total number of respondents	41	43	

Table 4. Frequency of use of metrics considered to have high diagnostic value by State programs.

[Frequencies are classified as first, second, or third priority. S, a richness-based metric; BI, biotic index; Z metric for which there was too little information provided to categorize adequately. EPT, Ephemeroptera, Plecoptera, Trichoptera; HBI, Hilsenhoff Biotic Index; FBI,-Family Biotic Index; NC, North Carolina. QSI, Quantitative Similarity Index; Max-X is from Hilsenhoff (1998)]

	Metric	First priority	Second priority	Third priority	Sum of top 3 cited metrics	Number of States citing metric
1	S – total	17	3	4	24	28
2	S – EPT	6	13	4	23	27
3	BI – HBI	3	1	4	8	19
4	% EPT	2		4	6	15
5	S – ephemeropterans	5	3	1	9	13
6	% of the dominant taxon					11
7	Diversity – Shannon	1		1	2	10
8	% ephemeropterans		1		1	9
9	% chironomids					8
10	% scrapers					8
11	S – trichopterans		2	2	4	8
12	S – plecopterans	1	1	4	6	8
13	% clingers					5
14	% non-insects			1	1	5
15	S – clingers					5
16	S – scrapers					5
17	% of the 2 most dominant taxa					4
18	BI		1	2	3	4
19	S – insects		3		3	4
20	% collectors					3
21	% predators		1		1	3
22	% tolerant individuals					3
23	BI – FBI		1		1	3
24	S – intolerant					3
25	% trichopterans					2
26	% EPT/(EPT + chironomids)					2

31

	Metric	First priority	Second priority	Third priority	Sum of top 3 cited metrics	Number of States citing metric
27	% nutrient tolerant individuals			1	1	2
28	% sensitive EPT					2
29	% plecopterans			1	1	2
30	% Tanytarsini					2
31	Abundance – total	2			2	2
32	BI – NC	2			2	2
33	S – coleopterans		1		1	2
34	S – dipterans			1	1	2
35	S – EPT % richness					2
36	S – filterers	1			1	2
37	S – genus		2		2	2
38	% – scrapers / filterers					1
39	% burrowers					1
40	% trichopterans - *Hydropsyche*					1
41	% chironomids + oligochaetes					1
42	% chironomids + tubificids + naidids					1
43	% climbers					1
44	% composition					1
45	% dipterans					1
46	% EPT index					1
47	% EPT / (EPT + chironomids)					1
48	% EPT / chironomids					1
49	% EPT - *Cheumatopsyche*					1
50	% filterers					1
51	% functional similarity to reference condition					1
52	% Hydropsychidae					1
53	% insects			1	1	1
54	% intolerant individuals					1
55	% isopods + snails + leeches					1
56	% model affinity					1
57	% mussels					1
58	% native atyid shrimp / abs					1

32

	Metric	First priority	Second priority	Third priority	Sum of top 3 cited metrics	Number of States citing metric
59	% non-*Hydropsyche* / total trichopteran abundance					1
60	% non-*Hydropsyche* trichopterans					1
61	% of the 3 most dominant taxa					1
62	% of the most frequent ffg					1
63	% oligochaetes			1	1	1
64	% oligochaetes + chironomids					1
65	% other dipterans + non-insects					1
66	% reference affinity					1
67	% scrapers / filterers					1
68	% shredders					1
69	% sprawlers			1	1	1
70	% plecopterans + trichopterans - *Hydropsyche*					1
71	% structural similarity to reference condition					1
72	% surface air breathers					1
73	% swimmers					1
74	% taxa richness					1
75	% tolerant urban					1
76	% total taxa S					1
77	Abundance – *Hydropsyche*					1
78	Abundance – sensitive		1		1	1
79	Abundance – plecopterans			1	1	1
80	Abundance of alien mollusks					1
81	Abundance of amphipods					1
82	Abundance of ephemeropterans					1
83	BI – Beck's					1
84	BI – Biological Condition Gradient taxa					1
85	BI – EPT					1
86	BI – Kansas family					1
87	BI – Kansas genus/species					1
88	BI – nutrient					1
89	BI – QSI					1
90	Diversity – Evenness		1		1	1

	Metric	First priority	Second priority	Third priority	Sum of top 3 cited metrics	Number of States citing metric
91	S – burrowers		1		1	1
92	S – chironomids					1
93	S – non-chironomid / oligochaete richness					1
94	S – non-insect					1
95	S – non-insect % richness					1
96	S – predators		1		1	1
97	S – scraper % richness					1
98	S – semivoltine (- coleopterans)					1
99	S – sensitive			1	1	1
100	S – sensitive families (Plains)					1
101	S – shredders			1	1	1
102	S – sprawlers					1
103	S – swimmers					1
104	S – tolerant					1
105	S – tolerant EPT		1		1	1
106	S – dipteran % richness					1
107	Z – Community loss					1
108	Z – Elmidae					1
109	Z – Functional Feeding Group					1
110	Z – Impact source determination					1
111	Z – Max-x			1	1	1
112	Z – Presence of crayfish					1

34

Table 5. Importance of each category of metric weighed by the priority given by State programs.

[See the Methods section for an explanation of the weighting procedure]

Metric	Weighted by priority	Percentage of total
Richness	1189	47.4
Percent of composition	853	34.0
Biotic index	309	12.3
Diversity	85	3.4
Abundance	75	3.0
Total		100.0

Table 6. Two-way contingency table indicating the difference between the use of sensitivity or tolerance metrics compared to functional feeding group and habitat metrics, east and west of the Mississippi River.

Location	Sensitivity and tolerance		Stream function and habitat		Row totals
	Hilsenhoff Biotic Index	Sensitivity or tolerance	Functional feeding group	Habitat	
East	15	10	11	6	42
West	7	6	20	11	44
Column Totals	22	16	31	17	86

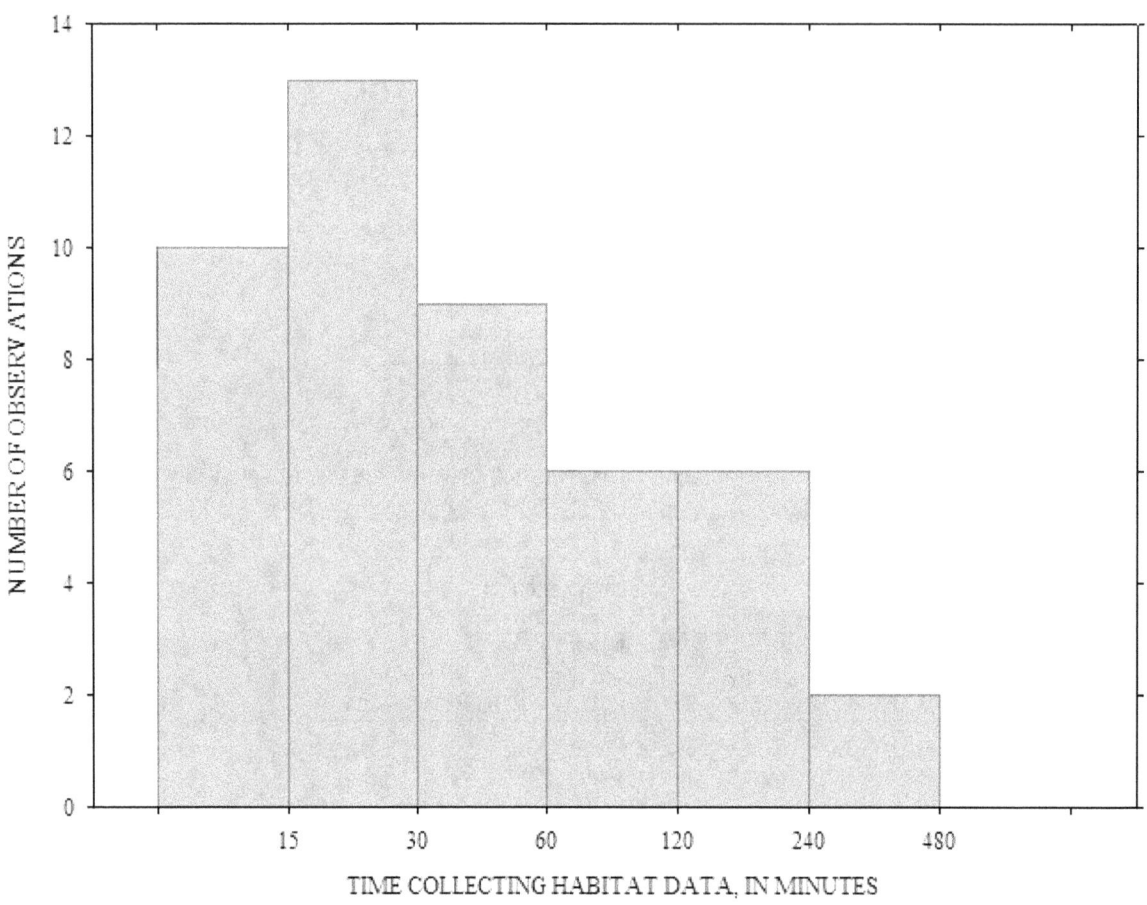

Figure 1. Histogram indicating the amount of time States spent collecting habitat data.

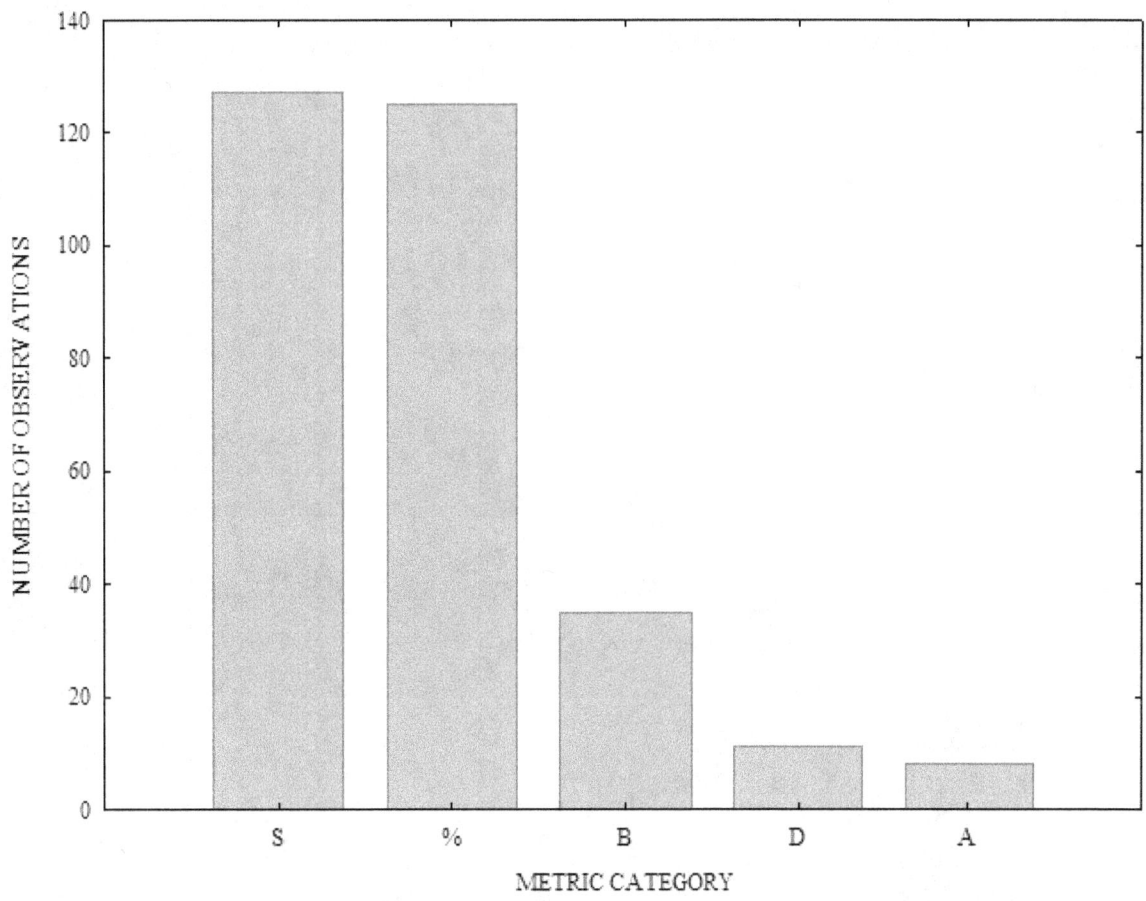

METRIC CATEGORY

Figure 2. The frequency of responses indicating the use of five categories of metrics. S, richness; %, percentage composition; B, biotic index; D, diversity; A, abundance.

This page left intentionally blank

Appendix 1. Survey

SECTION A: INITIAL QUESTIONS ON PURPOSE AND DESIGN

****

This section is designed to collect general data on the purpose(s) of your program and the analyses you use. It also asks basic questions regarding the collection of habitat data and other physical and chemical data. In this section, we also ask how you identify reference sites as well as how you partition the natural geographical variability in your state.

****

A-I. What is the principal purpose of your program? Although there can be many different purposes for collecting benthic data, please list your purposes in decreasing order of importance to the main goals of your program.

_____

_____

_____

_____

_____

_____

A-II. Given that most programs are under continuous development and therefore have an ongoing research component, and that most programs have multiple responsibilities, please rank how the analyses you describe below are used? **Please rank in order of importance with 1 equaling the most important.**

	Rank
A. Research	_____
B. Regulatory – Federal	_____
C. Regulatory – State	_____
D. Regulatory – Local	_____
E. Biotic index development	_____
F. RIVPACS-type development	_____
G. State-based biodiversity database	_____
H. Other (Please describe)	

_____

_____

_____

****

Programs often use different methods for analyzing point source compared to non-point source studies. Because there often are significant differences in study design between these two types of studies, we would greatly appreciate you filling out a separate questionnaire for point source as well as non-point source designs. Again, we realize the time it takes to complete the survey; however, we want to provide as complete a description of the methods currently being used as possible.

****

A-III. Are the analyses represented by your responses to this questionnaire used to determine point source or non-point source impairment? If neither, please describe in "Other". If both, briefly describe major differences in the analyses, if any.

    A. Point source impairment
    B. Non-point source impairment
    C. Other **(Please describe)**

_____
_____
_____

A-IV. Please identify whether the results of these analyses are currently used for the following purposes. If the results have not yet been used for one of the listed purposes, please estimate when you anticipate using them for each purpose, if ever.

	Yes	No	Estimated Date
A. Identifying designated use	___	___	_____
B. 303d listing	___	___	_____
C. 305b listing	___	___	_____
D. Establishing TMDLs	___	___	_____
E. Monitoring TMDLs	___	___	_____

F. Other **(please describe)** _____

_____
_____
_____

A-V. If you already have established biological criteria based on macroinvertebrates for the above purposes, are the criteria narrative and/or numeric? If you **do not** have narrative or numeric criteria, please estimate when you believe you will have established criteria.

	Narrative	Numeric
A. Identifying designated use	_____	_____
B. 303d listing	_____	_____
C. 305b listing	_____	_____
D. Establishing TMDLs	_____	_____

A-VI. Is your program sufficiently established such that when you collect a sample, the sample can be processed, analyzed statistically and immediately classified into an impairment category or ranked on an impairment gradient?   **Yes No**

****

The following few questions address general study design. The questions inquire about reference sites, partitioning your state into physiographic or biological regions and whether you collect replicates.

Identifying reference sites or a reference condition is often a complex process and there are a great variety of approaches used for identifying and defining reference sites. At one end of the scale, a reference site might be a single reach in a point-source study. Conversely, in large-scale studies a reference condition might be established by integrating the conditions at many reference sites. To be as succinct as possible, we only use the term reference site instead of both reference site and reference condition. We also realize there is a complex terminology associated with the term reference (Stoddard, J.L. et al. 2006. Ecological Applications), but in any event we assume you are using the best sites you have available as reference sites.
****

A-VII. Do you have established reference sites?

    Yes   No

If yes,

    A. How many do you have in your entire state? _____

    B. Do you stratify your reference sites based on broad geographic categories and/or by other criteria (e.g., ecoregion, physiographic region, land use/cover types, altitude, stream order) as an aid in analyzing your macroinvertebrate data?

        Yes   No

If yes, please list from most important to least important up to 5 factors you consider during the stratification process.

        A. _____

        B. _____

        C. _____

        D. _____

        E. _____

    C. Who chose or established your reference site(s)?

        1. You and your staff

        2. Other agency

        3. Consultant

        4. Your predecessor(s)

    D. Are reference sites chosen based only on physical and chemical data (i.e., not using benthic invertebrate data)?

        Yes   No

If yes,

    1. What factor(s) are used to determine that a site is a reference site?

    Please circle all that apply.

        a. Physical habitat attributes of the site

        b. Chemical attributes of the site

        c. A multivariate construct composed of information from habitat, physical, and chemical data.

        d. GIS-derived land cover and land use data.

        e. Best Professional Judgment (BPJ)

        f. None of the above **(please describe)** _____

        _____

        _____

        _____

If no:
> **That is, sites are not chosen using physical/chemical data alone,**

> 2. Are sites chosen based on benthic macroinvertebrate composition alone?　**Yes**　**No**

> 3. Are sites chosen based on a combination of physical, chemical and macroinvertebrate data?　**Yes**　**No**

> > **If yes, please shortly describe the method used**:
> > _____
> > _____

If no distinct reference sites are used,
> E. Do you establish reference sites based on other methods such as from a gradient of least impaired to the most impaired sites?　**Yes**　**No**

> > **If yes, please describe:** _____
> > _____
> > _____

A-VIII. Do you have reference sites in common with other benthic invertebrate sampling programs?
> **Yes**　**No**

If yes,
> A. Is the program in another state?　**Yes**　**No**
> B. Is the program a federal program (e.g., NAWQA, EMAP, WSA)
> **Yes**　　　**No**

If yes, please describe: _____
_____
_____

****

Establishing what constitutes a replicate in lotic assessments can be problematic. In small-scale studies separate collections at a site are often considered replicates. In larger scale studies, individual sites may be considered replicates. Please answer the following questions as best you can.

****

A-IX. Do you collect replicates?　　**Yes**　**No**

If yes,
> A. Do you consider multiple collections from the same site replicates? (Please do not include single collections that are eventually composited as being replicates)　**Yes**　**No**

> > **If yes, how many replicates per site are collected:** _____
> > **If no,**
> B. Do you consider collections from different sites as replicates?
> > **Yes**　**No**

> > **If yes, how many replicates are collected:** _____

> > **If no, briefly described what you consider a replicate to be:** _____
> > _____
> > _____

42

A-X. Is your method of collecting benthic invertebrates based on: **(Please circle only one)**
   A. A fixed area
   B. A fixed effort (e.g., equal number of jabs, equal time period)
   C. Qualitative (e.g., sampling for maximum richness)

Please describe why you chose A, B, or C. _____

_____

_____

_____

_____

SECTION B: QA/QC AND CONTRACTOR INFORMATION

****

Some state programs identify macroinvertebrates using in-house personnel while other programs contract out this task. This section will help us determine where samples are processed and what QA/QC procedures are followed.
****

B-I. Regardless of whether your samples are identified in-house or by a contractor, have all individuals performing identifications been fully certified by the North American Benthological Society's Taxonomic Certification Program for those organisms they are identifying?
   Yes   No

****

B-II. Are all or most of your samples processed by a contractor?
   Yes   No

If yes, continue to B-III; if no, please go to B-V

B-III. Does the contractor calculate the metrics you use in your analyzes?   Yes   No

B-IV. Does the contractor assign estimates of site quality?   Yes   No

****

B-V. Are the samples retained after analysis?
   Yes No
If yes,
      A. By you
      B. By the contractor
      C. No

B-VI. Is a reference collection maintained?
    Yes No
If yes,
      A. By you
      B. By the contractor
      C. No

B-VII. Is a voucher collection specific to a study maintained?   **Yes No**

If yes,

    A. By you

    B. By the contractor

    C. No

B-VIII. Are any identifications reviewed or confirmed by an outside party?

    Yes No

If yes, (please circle and fill in only one)

    A. What percentage of samples is reviewed? _____

    OR

    B. What percentage of individual organisms is reviewed? _____

    OR

    C. Only taxa that are uncertain are reviewed?

B-IX. Once the samples are sorted and identified, are the counts per taxon checked?

    Yes No

If yes,

    A. What percentage of samples is checked? _____

OR

    B. What percentage of individuals is checked? _____

OR

    C. What percentage of taxa is reviewed? _____

SECTION C: HABITAT DATA COLLECTION

****

The measurement of physical and chemical habitat is an integral part of many bioassessment programs. Habitat measurements can include visual estimates of stream condition or extensive, detailed quantitative measurements. A wide range of effort among programs exists and effort is often a function of the questions being addressed. We can't begin to list all the factors measured during habitat assessments; however, we would like to know which measures are most often made.

****

C-I. Do you collect on-site habitat data?   **Yes No**

If yes,

    A. Do you use the EPA Visual Habitat Assessment Protocol (Barbour et. al. 1999)? **Yes No**

    B. Is the same protocol used throughout your state? **Yes No**

    C. Do you use a protocol that is only specific to your program? **Yes No**

    D. Please estimate the time spent per site collecting habitat data? _____

If no,

    E. Do you obtain habitat data from another source/agency?

    Yes   No

    Please describe:_____

_____

_____

_____

C-II. Do you also collect any of the follow site specific data? (**please circle**)

A. water velocity

B. stream depth   **(Please circle: wetted and/or bankfull)**

C. stream width   **(Please circle: wetted and/or bankfull)**

D. discharge

E. Wolman pebble counts   **(Please circle number per count: 100 50 other** _____ **)**

F. Temperature   **(Please circle: Air   Water)**

C-III. Do you also collect on-site chemical data?   **Yes   No**

If yes, (please circle)

    A. Dissolved oxygen

    B. pH

    C. Conductivity

    D. Hardness

    E. Nutrients (please list) _____

_____

    F. Other (please list) _____

_____

_____

_____

C-IV. Do you have access to continuous monitoring data, such as discharge, temperature, water chemistry that can be used to associate with your benthic invertebrate samples?   **Yes   No**

If yes, please briefly describe how you use these continuous data:

_____

_____

_____

C-V. Do you use land use or land cover data (e.g., NLCD [National Land Cover Data] and/or state data) during the analysis of your data?

    Yes   No

If yes, please briefly describe how you use these data:

_____

_____

_____

SECTION D: BENTHIC MACROINVERTEBRATE DATA PREPARATION

****

Prior to data analysis per se, many decisions are made regarding which taxonomic groups to use, how richness-based metrics are estimated, whether data are standardized or transformed, etc. Making these choices is further complicated because different metrics and/or analytical methods are variously sensitive to these manipulations. This section inquires whether you use some of the most common procedures.

****

D-I. Please list the major taxonomic groups (e.g., worms, mites, midges, terrestrials insects) that you omit from the analyses.

_____

_____

D-II. Do you use taxonomic attributes (= species traits, e.g., functional feeding group designations, tolerance scores) in your analyses?

Yes   No

If yes,

Please indicate whether the following attributes are used and your source(s) of information:

	Merritt & Cummins	Barbour et al. 1999	Local Expertise	Other (Describe)
Functional Feeding Groups				
Habit (clinger, sprawler, etc.)				
Habitat (e.g., erosional, depostional)				
Tolerance to organic loading				
Tolerance to metals				

Please list additional species traits and/or tolerance information used and source(s) of information: _____

_____

_____

_____

_____

D-III. If a taxon does not have a "known" tolerance value, do you assign a tolerance value to it prior to your analyses?

Yes   No

If yes,

Please indicate which of the following you do:

    A. Assign a tolerance value of a related taxon at the same taxonomic level (e.g., assign Fallceon the value that Baetis has).

    B. Assign a tolerance value of the next higher taxon (e.g., assign Fallceon the tolerance value of Baetidae).

    C. Do not use the information for the taxon that is missing a assigned tolerance value.

    D. Other **(please describe)** _____

_____

_____

_____

****

D-IV. Datasets of benthic invertebrates often contain many "rare" taxa; however, no generally accepted definition of rare exists. The following questions address some issues involving rare taxa.

    A. Do you modify your data in any fashion to deal with rare taxa? **Yes   No**
    If no, please go to question D-V, if yes please continue.

    B. How do you define rare?
        1. Individuals of a taxon represent less than a fixed percentage of the sample **(please list %)** _____
        2. Individuals of a taxon represent less than a fixed percentage of the study **(please list %)** _____
        3. A taxon (regardless of the number of individuals) occurs in less than a fixed percentage of the samples **(please list %)** _____
        4. A taxon occurs at less than a fixed percentage of the sites **(please list %)** _____
        5. A taxon contains less than or equal to a certain number of individuals (e.g., 1) **(please list number)** _____
    C. Briefly describe why you may delete rare taxa. _____

_____

_____

D-V. Do you subsample by selecting a fixed-count of individuals.
Yes   No
If yes,

    A. What is your target number of individuals to sort (please list) _____

    B. What is the maximum acceptable number of organisms sorted that you will include in your analyses? (Please list) _____

    C. What is your minimum acceptable number of organisms sorted that you will include in your analyses? (Please list) _____

    D. Although subsampling by sorting a fixed count of individuals is a form of rarefying, do you further rarify your samples by computer before evaluating measures of richness?
    Yes   No

D-VI. Do you subsample randomly? **Yes   No**
If yes,

    A. Do you also sort large and rare individuals to use in your data analyses?
    Yes   No

D-VII. How many metrics to you commonly calculate for each analysis? _____.

Please list 10 or fewer of the metrics you find most useful. Please list from most useful to least useful. Also, if specific transformations are used prior to analyzing the metric, please list the transformation.

	Metric	Transformation
1.	_____	_____
2.	_____	_____
3.	_____	_____
4.	_____	_____
5.	_____	_____
6.	_____	_____
7.	_____	_____
8.	_____	_____
9.	_____	_____
10.	_____	_____

D-VIII. Do you calculate a multimetric index or score? **Yes   No**

D-IX. Do you commonly report density (individuals/area) as a metric?   **Yes   No**

SECTION E: STATISTICAL CALCULATIONS
****
Programs use a combination of statistical techniques which include univariate, bivariate, and multivariate statistics. The following questions address factors associated with their use.
****

E-I. Do you perform statistical calculations on your data?   **Yes   No**

If yes, please list the names of the statistical package(s) (=software) that you use most often.
_____
_____
_____

E-II. What are the 5 most common non-multivariate statistical techniques (t-tests, ANOVA, correlation, regression) you use for analyzing your benthic invertebrate data? **(Please list from most often to least often used)**

A. _____

B. _____

C. _____

D. _____

E. _____

E-III. Do you use RIVPACS or RIVPACS-type analyses? **Yes   No**

E-IV. Do you use classification and ordination techniques for analyzing your data? Yes No
If yes, please list the names of the classification and ordination packages (=software) you use.
(Please list from most often to least often used)

    A. _____

    B. _____

    C. _____

    D. _____

    E. _____

E-V. Please list the 5 most often used ordination and classification techniques (e.g., PCA, DCA, CCA, TWINSPAN, UPGMA) along with (dis)similarity measures (Jaccard, Bray-Curtis, etc) if appropriate. **(Please list from most-to-least used)**

    A. _____
_____

    B. _____
_____

    C. _____
_____

    D. _____
_____

    E. _____

    F. _____

E-VI. Although there are many transformations and weights that can be used in the multivariate analysis of macroinvertebrate data, please indicate the methods most often used by ranking the list below from 1 = most often used to n = least often used.

    A. Generally don't modify data   _____

    B. Log transformation of abundance   _____

    C. Square-root of abundance   _____

    D. Double square-root of abundance   _____

    E. Conversion to % per sample   _____

    F. Conversion to presence-absence   _____

    G. Elimination of rare taxa   _____

    H. Down-weighting rare taxa   _____

    I. Other **(please list)** _____
_____
_____

SECTION F: DATA STORAGE

****

Data storage is often one of the last aspects of bioassessment programs that are developed. Unfortunately, most biologists are ill prepared to deal with this aspect of data analysis. Biomonitoring data, in particular, habitat data storage can be extremely challenging. Efficient data analysis is highly dependent on an effective database system.

****

F-I. Do you store your data in electronic form? Yes No
If yes,

      A. Are the data stored in a:
          1. flat file (ASCII)

          2. spreadsheet **(please list)** _____

          3. database **(please list)** _____

      B. Are the data available on the Internet to others? **Yes**   **No**

F-II. Are your data also systematically stored in hardcopy? **Yes**   **No**

F-III. What is (are) the principal source(s) (Merritt & Cummins, Integrated Taxonomic Information System (ITIS), Zoological Record etc.) for the nomenclature you use in your database? (Please list)

_____
_____
_____
_____
_____

F-IV. Given that many programs have existed for a decade or more, do you update historic data?
      Yes   **No**
If yes, (please circle all that apply)

      A. To account for changes in nomenclature?
      B. Identify previously unknown taxa?
      C. Split and/or lump previously identified taxa as the science and/or your taxonomic expertise develops?

CONCLUSION

Thank you very much for filling out our questionnaire. The data derived from this survey will allow all of us to better understand the techniques and methods currently used for analyzing benthic macroinvertebrate samples.

www.ingramcontent.com/pod-product-compliance
Lightning Source LLC
Chambersburg PA
CBHW080445290526
45791CB00008BA/2608